Table of Contents

Introduction

Types of Stories

- traditional tall tales
- original tall tales

Ways to Use the Stories

1. Directed lessons
   - with small groups of students who are reading at the same level
   - with an individual student
   - with the whole class to support a unit of study

2. Partner reading

3. Cooperative learning groups

4. Independent practice
   - at school
   - at home

Things to Consider

1. Determine your purpose for selecting a story—instructional device, partner reading, group work, or independent reading. Varying purposes call for different degrees of story difficulty.

2. A single story may be used for more than one purpose. You might first use a story as an instructional tool, have partners read the story a second time for greater fluency, and then use the story at a later time for independent reading.

3. When presenting a story to a group or an individual for the first time, review any vocabulary that will be difficult to decode or understand. Many students will benefit from a review of the vocabulary page and the questions before they read the story.

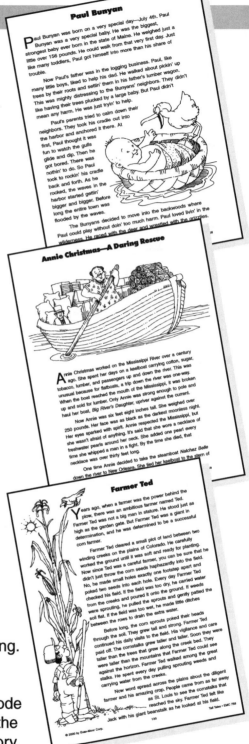

Types of Skill Pages

Three or four pages of activities covering a variety of reading skills follow each story:

- comprehension
- vocabulary
- structural analysis
- parts of speech
- categorizing
- literary analysis

Ways to Use Skill Pages

1. Individualize skill practice for each student with tasks that are appropriate for his or her needs.

2. As directed minilessons, the skill pages may be used in several ways:

   - Make a transparency for students to follow as you work through the lesson.

   - Write the activity on the board and call on students to fill in the answers.

   - Reproduce the page for everyone to use as you direct the lesson.

3. When using the skill pages for independent practice, make sure that the skills have been introduced to the reader. Review the directions and check for understanding. Review the completed lesson with the students to determine if further practice is needed.

Engineer Red and Sooner Hound

Sooner Hound was a big dog. He was white with bright red spots. He had long, thin legs and a long tail with a curl in the middle. He had big, floppy ears that would swing from side to side like the pendulum on a grandfather clock as he ran. That dog would sooner run than eat. He would sooner eat than sleep. So he would sooner run than anything. He was the fastest thing on four legs.

Now Sooner Hound belonged to an engineer named Red. The hound ran alongside the train as it chugged down the tracks. Just as the train would pull into a station, Sooner Hound would pass the train. He would leap onto the platform and wait for Red to stop the engine.

Red and Sooner Hound were an inseparable pair. Wherever Red's engine went, Sooner Hound ran alongside the train. Sometimes it was tiresome for the hound to go as slowly as the train. He would run ahead. Then he would play around in the fields and scare up a rabbit or two until the train caught up.

One time a new stationmaster saw Red and Sooner Hound and stopped the pair. "Hey there, Red. It's against the rules for a dog to ride on the train. You'll have to leave that hound here at the station."

"Shucks!" Red replied. "Sooner doesn't ride, he just runs along beside the train!"

"You mean to say he keeps up with the train?" the stationmaster asked.

"Oh, no," Red answered. "Most of the time he runs up ahead of it. He gets to the station before I do. He just waits for me to arrive."

The stationmaster laughed so hard that he popped the buttons off his shirt. "Red, you're the biggest yarn-teller in the county. There ain't never been a dog that can keep up with a train. Let Sooner Hound go along on today's run. If he gets to the station before you do, I'll buy you both the best dinner in town!"

"Suits me," said Red. "But I have to warn you, Sooner is the fastest thing on four legs."

Red pulled his engineer's cap onto his head and climbed into the engine. When the train pulled out of the station, Sooner Hound trotted beside it. Sooner didn't run. He didn't have to. The train was just too slow. To make the trip more interesting, Sooner decided to trot in big circles around the train. Of course, he got to the station long before the train.

The stationmaster couldn't believe his eyes. When the train did pull into the station, Sooner was loping easily around a tree. He was barking at a cat. Sooner didn't look even a mite tired. Well, that stationmaster had learned his lesson. He bought Red and Sooner Hound a very good dinner.

You may have seen dogs running beside the railroad tracks. But they never run as fast as the trains. That won't happen until another dog comes along like Red's fast Sooner Hound.

                                       Tall Tales • EMC 758

Name _____

Questions about
Engineer Red and Sooner Hound

1. What was unusual about what Sooner Hound liked to do?

_____

_____

2. What was unusual about how Sooner Hound looked?

_____

_____

3. How did Sooner Hound earn a dinner?

_____

_____

4. The tale says that Engineer Red and Sooner Hound were **an inseparable pair.** Explain what that statement means. Give an example from the tale that proves the statement is true.

_____

_____

_____

_____

_____

_____

Name _____

Engineer Red and Sooner Hound
Compound Words

A. Write the two words used to make each of these compound words.

1. grandfather   _____   _____

2. alongside   _____   _____

3. sometimes   _____   _____

4. stationmaster   _____   _____

5. railroad   _____   _____

B. Use the compound words above to complete these sentences.

1. _____ the _____ had to decide which

   engine could stay on the main tracks.

2. Many trains used the same _____ tracks.

3. My _____ told a story about a horse that ran

   _____ his horseless carriage.

C. Write your own sentence. Include at least one compound word.

_____

_____

Name _____

Engineer Red and Sooner Hound
Similes

A. Tell the two things that are being compared in this simile about Sooner Hound.

He had ears that could swing from side to side like the pendulum on a grandfather clock.

_____

B. Write sentences using similes to compare the pairs of things below.

1. Sooner Hound's spots—a child with the measles

_____

_____

2. Sooner Hound's tail—a cursive **e**

_____

_____

3. Sooner Hound's legs—stilts

_____

_____

4. Sooner Hound's speed—_____
(Think of something fast and write it here.)

_____

_____

Name _____

Engineer Red and Sooner Hound
Using Quotation Marks

A. Add quotation marks to these sentences to show what words were said.

1. Shucks! Red replied. Sooner doesn't ride. He just runs along beside the train!

2. Oh, no! Red answered. Most of the time he runs up ahead of it.

3. Suits me, said Red. But I have to warn you, Sooner is the fastest thing on four legs.

4. The new stationmaster said, Hey there, Red. It's against the rules for a dog to ride on the train.

B. Write a sentence of your own that tells something someone said. Use the quotation marks correctly.

_____

_____

C. Write the name of the character who said each thing.

_____   "You'll have to leave that hound here."

_____   "Sooner doesn't ride, he just runs alongside."

_____   "There ain't never been a dog that can keep up with a train."

_____   "Sooner is the fastest thing on four legs."

9   Tall Tales • EMC 758

Joe and Bess Call

Joe and Bess Call were brother and sister. They had a farm in Essex County, New York. When he was a young man, Joe had been a champion wrestler. He was known the world over for his strength. Bess was younger than her brother, a little shorter (not quite six feet), but nearly as strong. Bess looked as calm as vanilla ice cream. But when she was upset, she was dangerous.

Even though Joe had retired, young men often visited the Call farm to challenge him to a wrestling match. Sometimes Joe was able to explain that he no longer wrestled. Sometimes there was nothing to do but to pin them and send them on their way.

One hot summer day, a man came to the farm. He had traveled all the way from England to challenge Joe. He rode up the dirt road. Joe was talking with Bess. The team of oxen with the plow stood nearby. The Englishman asked them if they could tell him where Joe lived. Smiling, Joe lifted the plow in one hand and pointed down the road.

The man's face fell. "You must be Joe Call," he whispered. "I came here hoping to have a wrestling match with you, but I think, perhaps, this is not the best day for it."

"Hmmmm. It is a mighty hot day," Joe agreed.

The stranger turned tail and hurried back toward town. Bess grinned and said, "That feller's face fell longer than the well is deep!" Then she lifted up the plow and looked at the blade. "This blade is gettin' mighty dull. Let me sharpen it for you tonight."

Well, the Englishman did not give up. He went back to town and hired two trainers. He worked and worked to build up his strength. At the end of the summer, he could lift a plow over his head. Now he was ready to wrestle Joe Call. He went back to the Call farm.

Joe was not home. The Englishman found Bess sitting on the front porch. "I have come to wrestle Joe Call," the man announced.

"Joe isn't here today. I usually do the wrestlin' while Joe's away," Bess murmured.

The man chuckled at the thought of wrestling Joe's sister. The chuckle made Bess mad. She picked the man up and threw him off the porch. "I'll show you a wrestlin' match!" Bess shouted as she rolled up her sleeves.

It wasn't much of a contest. Bess seemed to have the upper hand from the first throw. The contest ended when she threw the Englishman and his horse over the fence into a muddy ditch.

Joe passed the mud-splattered visitor as he rode home from town. When he got to the farm, he asked Bess what had happened to the English fellow.

"Oh, he wanted to wrestle and I obliged," confided Bess. "He's a pretty poor loser. I didn't have the heart to tell him I was feelin' a mite under the weather today."

Tall Tales • EMC 758

Name _____

Questions about
Joe and Bess Call

1. What did Joe and Bess have in common?

_____

_____

2. What did the Englishman want to do?

_____

_____

3. Would you describe the Englishman as persistent? Explain why.

_____

_____

_____

4. Do you think Bess was calm? Give an example to support your answer.

_____

_____

_____

5. What clues did the storyteller use to let you know that Bess was really strong?

_____

_____

_____

Name _____

Joe and Bess Call
Vocabulary

A. Write the number of each word on the line in front of its meaning.

1. riled   _____ a contest

2. pin   _____ a sport

3. match   _____ to laugh

4. chuckle   _____ upset

5. wrestling   _____ to flatten to the ground

B. The phrases below are used in a special way in this tale. Use the tale's context to determine each meaning. Then write a definition for each phrase.

1. The stranger <u>turned tail</u> and hurried back to town.

_____

2. Bess was feeling <u>a mite under the weather</u>.

_____

3. The Englishman's <u>face fell</u>.

_____

Name _____

Joe and Bess Call
Vocabulary

A. The word **said** is often overused in writing. In the tall tale *Joe and Bess Call,* the storyteller used several different synonyms for **said**.

1. Look back at the tale and list four synonyms for **said**.

_____   _____

_____   _____

2. Add at least four of your own synonyms to the list.

_____   _____

_____   _____

B. Rewrite this sentence using four different synonyms for **said**.

Bess said that she was as strong as Joe.

_____

_____

_____

_____

C. Does the meaning of the sentence change when you change the words? _____
Give an example that supports your answer.

_____

_____

Name _____

Joe and Bess Call

Wrestling with a Problem

1. When you struggle with a decision, sometimes you say that you are "wrestling with the problem."

   What are the two things being compared?

   _____   _____

2. List the similarities and differences between the two.

   Similarities _____

   _____

   _____

   _____

   _____

   Differences _____

   _____

   _____

   _____

   _____

3. Think of a decision that you have had to make. On another sheet of paper, write about the struggle. Make it sound like a wrestling match.

15

How Pecos Bill Got His Name

Pecos Bill was raised by a coyote. In fact, he thought that he was a coyote until he was full-grown. You see when Bill was four, his family decided to move west from Texas. His pa loaded the family—Ma and all seventeen children—into an old covered wagon. Bill's ma and pa sat on the seat at the front of the wagon and all the children rode in the back. The noise that those children made was louder than a giant clap of thunder rattlin' in a big black cloud.

Just as the wagon was about to ford the Pecos River, it bounced over a rock on the trail. Bill bounced out and landed on a pile of sand. It wasn't until the wagon stopped for the noonday meal that the red-haired boy was missed. Bill's ma and pa and all of his brothers and sisters searched the trail. But there was no sign of a little boy. The last that anyone could remember seeing Bill was just before the wagon had crossed the Pecos River. After that, whenever anyone thought of Bill, they thought of the river too. That's when they began to call him Pecos Bill.

Well now, Bill had been rescued, but not by a human. It was a kind coyote that took Bill home. The coyote taught Bill the ways of the wilderness. Bill was a fast learner. It wasn't long before he knew all the secrets of hunting. He could find a field mouse in its nest. He knew where the thrush hid her eggs and where the squirrels stored their nuts. He could leap long distances and run for hours without tiring. He spoke the language of the coyote and understood each of the wild beasts. Every night he sat with his coyote family. They yipped and howled at the sky.

Bill was a striking beast. His skin was a shiny dark brown from his hours in the sun. His long, uncombed red hair fell over his shoulders. Strong muscles rippled on his arms and legs.

One afternoon, a wandering cowboy happened upon Bill. The wild man was sitting by the edge of the Pecos River. The two stared at each other in wonder. Bill had never seen a man. The cowboy had never seen a wild creature like this one. They circled each other warily. Bill yelped and began to run away. The cowboy mimicked the yelps and stood his ground.

For nearly a month the cowboy and Bill wandered around each other. They shared meals of the meat that Bill dragged in from the kill. They drank from the clear stream. It was there, when they were drinking together, that Bill first looked at his reflection. He saw how he was like the man.

Pecos Bill, the wild coyote-man, found out he was really a human. And the cowboy? He was one of Bill's long-lost brothers. In the end, Bill was reunited with his family. He went on to become one of the most famous cowboys who had lived.

Tall Tales • EMC 758

Name _____

Questions about
How Pecos Bill Got His Name

1. What was unusual about Pecos Bill's childhood?

_____

_____

2. How did Pecos Bill get his name?

_____

_____

3. What important lessons did Pecos Bill learn from the coyote?

_____

_____

4. When did Pecos Bill discover he was not a coyote?

_____

_____

5. What two things made the cowboy's discovery of Pecos Bill especially amazing?

_____

_____

_____

_____

Name _____

How Pecos Bill Got His Name

Vocabulary

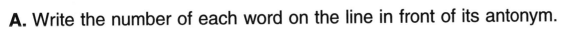

A. Write the number of each word on the line in front of its antonym.

    1. loaded   _____ short

    2. stop   _____ unloaded

    3. fast   _____ uncombed

    4. long   _____ slow

    5. combed   _____ found

    6. hot   _____ cold

    7. lost   _____ go

B. Choose words from the lists above to complete these sentences so they tell about the tale.

    1. Pa _____ his family into the wagon.

    2. It was a _____ time before Bill's family missed him.

    3. The wild man had brown skin and _____ hair.

    4. The cowboy was one of Bill's long-_____ brothers.

 Tall Tales • EMC 758

Name _____

How Pecos Bill Got His Name
Making Comparisons

A. The story says that Pecos Bill and his brothers and sisters were "louder than a giant clap of thunder rattlin' in a big black cloud." Make a list of six loud noises.

_____   _____

_____   _____

_____   _____

B. Write the noises in order from softest to loudest.

1._____   4._____

2._____   5._____

3._____   6._____

C. Complete these sentences comparing different noises.

Example: When <u>the boy yelled</u>, it was louder than <u>a pen of snorting pigs</u>.

When _____, it was louder than _____.

When _____, it was louder than _____.

When _____, it was louder than _____.

20   Tall Tales • EMC 758

Name _____

How Pecos Bill Got His Name
Sequencing Story Events

Number the story events in the correct order.

_____ Bill sat with his family and yipped and howled at the sky.

_____ The cowboy stared at the wild creature.

_____ Bill's pa loaded the family into a covered wagon.

_____ Bill learned the secrets of hunting.

_____ The wagon bounced over a rock on the trail.

_____ Bill looked into the clear stream and saw his reflection.

_____ Bill bounced out of the wagon.

_____ Bill was reunited with his family.

Pecos Bill and the Twister

Pecos Bill was the gall-darndest cowboy there ever was. He could ride any critter. He could swing his rope with deadeye aim. Take that time during a hot summer when the prairie was

parched by the sun. Herds of cattle stood at the dry creek beds with their tongues lolling out of their mouths. Pecos Bill lassoed a grove of prickly-pear cactuses. He pulled them back and forth to dig out a canal. Then he lassoed a bend of the Rio Grande. He pulled the river and tipped it into the empty canal.

Here is a story about one of his famous roping feats.

One day a black funnel moved across the prairie. It raced across the ground. Pecos Bill, on his horse Widow Maker, rode straight toward the oncoming storm. The cowboys couldn't believe their eyes. Now they had seen Bill do incredible things. They knew that he was not afraid of anything. But this time it seemed that Bill had met his match. Pecos Bill unfurled his lariat. He whirled its loop above his head. He hurled the loop at the head of the storm. Pecos Bill had roped the twister! The next moment the men saw Pecos leap headlong into the air. He disappeared in the blackness. Widow Maker shied to one side just in time to miss the swirling storm.

The storm had passed. The cowboys searched for Pecos Bill. They felt sure that he had been thrown to the ground by the swirling black funnel. They could see the tracks the twister left. It had reared off the earth when Pecos Bill got his noose around its neck. They all agreed that there was no better rider than Pecos Bill. But no one believed that Pecos Bill could have survived a Texas twister.

As his men looked for his remains, Pecos Bill was having the time of his life. He was riding through the sky. The twister tore across the desert. It cakewalked and twisted worse than a herd of bucking broncos. The twister bucked and turned trying to shake Pecos Bill off its back. It tore up trees and rocks. It threw them at the figure on its back. Pecos dodged the debris and held fast. The rain caused by the windstorm fell fast. It flooded the gully that the twister had created. Quick as a wink the Grand Canyon was created.

Now Pecos Bill was an experienced bronco buster. He knew when he was about to lose his seat. He decided to dismount! He looked hard in every direction for a safe place to jump. When he saw a soft, sandy desert below him, he let go. As he landed, sand splashed out on all sides like a wave in the ocean. Bill found himself in a deep bowl of sand. He had splashed out a huge hole in the desert. That hole later became known as Death Valley.

Well, Pecos Bill finally made his way back to his ranch. The cowboys marveled at his latest feat. Pecos Bill was no ordinary buckaroo.

Name _____

Questions about
Pecos Bill and the Twister

1. What natural phenomenon inspired this tall tale?

   _____

2. What animal is compared to the twister? Cite some examples from the story that support your conclusion.

   _____

   _____

3. What two famous landmarks are referred to in this tale?

   _____

4. What skills might be important to a cowboy?

   _____

   _____

   _____

5. What was the name of Pecos Bill's horse? Why do you think that was its name?

   _____

   _____

   _____

6. On another sheet of paper, tell whether you agree with the storyteller's observation that "Pecos Bill was the gall-darndest cowboy there ever was." Support your answer.

24

Name _____

Pecos Bill and the Twister
Vocabulary

A. This tale uses many words and phrases that have special meanings. Write the number of each word or phrase on the line in front of the meaning that it has in the tale.

1. gall-darndest   _____ hanging loosely

2. deadeye aim   _____ raised on hind legs

3. lolling out   _____ accurate

4. bronco buster   _____ found an equal

5. met his match   _____ most amazing

6. reared   _____ horse trainer

B. Show that you understand what each of the underlined phrases mean by answering the questions.

1. What can you do <u>quick as a wink</u>?

   _____

2. What would you <u>leap headlong</u> into?

   _____

3. What would make you <u>shy away</u>?

   _____

Name _____

Pecos Bill and the Twister
Comparing Two Things

In order to make the comparison between two things, authors sometimes use special words associated with one of the things to describe the other. Choose the best meaning for the underlined words in each sentence. Then write the name of the thing usually associated with those words.

1. The twister <u>cakewalked and twisted</u> across the sky.

   ○ strolled through a bakery   ○ bucked and spun around   ○ tiptoed

   Cowboys use the word **cakewalked** to tell about a _____.

2. Pecos Bill <u>mounted</u> the twister.

   ○ put in a frame   ○ hiked up   ○ got onto

   Equestrians talk about **mounting** a _____.

3. The sand <u>splashed</u> out on all sides.

   ○ got wet   ○ painted   ○ went over the edge

   People use the word **splash** when they are talking about _____.

4. The twister <u>reared</u> off the ground.

   ○ stood only on its hind legs   ○ rose up   ○ parented

   Most often, the word **rear** means a _____ is standing on its hind legs and lifting its front legs off the ground.

Name _____

Pecos Bill and the Twister
Crossword Puzzle

Word Box

boss

yahoo

rope

rio

horse

cowboy

ranch

valley

drought

pear

twister

Across

3. a cattle herder

7. Widow Maker

9. A prickly-_____ is a type of cactus.

11. a long period without rain

Down

1. a Spanish word for river

2. a violent windstorm

4. a cowboy exclamation

5. a low area between hills

6. a strong, thick cord

8. a cattle-grazing establishment

10. the one in charge

Tall Tales • EMC 758

Slue-Foot Sue

Slue-Foot Sue was one of the great ladies of the Texas frontier. She was about as famous as her Texas cowboy husband, Pecos Bill. Slue-Foot Sue met Bill when she was riding past his ranch. She was on the back of the world's largest catfish. It was love at first sight! Bill proposed marriage on the spot. Sue said that she would marry Bill on two conditions. First, she wanted a brand-new, store-bought wedding dress with a bustle. Second, she wanted to ride Bill's horse, Widow Maker, to the wedding.

Bill rode nonstop to Dallas that very afternoon. He picked up the prettiest wedding dress you ever did see. Meeting the second condition wasn't quite as easy. Bill knew Sue was a mighty good rider. But no one besides Bill had ever ridden Widow Maker before.

Sue dressed in the beautiful gown. She mounted Widow Maker. Sue's bustle touched the powerful animal's back. Widow Maker bucked. Sue was blasted clean out of the saddle and into space. She fell back to the ground. Her store-bought bustle was like a spring. She must have bounced off the ground twenty times before Bill was able to lasso her.

During this unplanned space trip, Sue found a solution to a really big problem. You see, Texas was in the middle of a terrible, great drought. The drought had lasted so long that children didn't even know what rain was. It was so dry that spit disappeared before it ever hit the ground. All the cattle walked around with their tongues hanging out. They made puny, little coughing noises.

Sue directed Bill to gather up lots of rope. She climbed with Bill to the highest mountain on their ranch. They set to work tying all the ropes together. They made the longest lasso anyone had ever seen.

Sue pointed to the Little Dipper. She told Pecos Bill to lasso the handle of the constellation. Bill began to spin the loop of his lasso larger and larger, faster and faster. Finally he let it go. It went streaking into the sky. Bill and Sue waited for hours. At last the loop of the lasso found the handle of the Little Dipper. Bill and Sue pulled and tugged on the end of the lasso all through the night. Finally the dipper began to tip toward the earth.

The first rays of the morning sun peeked over the horizon. The water from the Little Dipper began to spill toward the earth. The great Texas drought was finally at an end—thanks to Slue-Foot Sue, her bustle, and her out-of-this-world ride.

Name _____

Questions about
Slue-Foot Sue

1. What two conditions did Sue have for marrying Pecos Bill?

_____

_____

2. Why do you think Bill's horse was named Widow Maker?

_____

_____

3. What was the unexpected outcome of Sue's ride on Widow Maker?

_____

_____

4. How dry was it in Texas when the story took place? Give three examples that tell how dry it was.

_____

_____

_____

5. What was Slue-Foot Sue's plan to end the drought in Texas? Write a step-by-step plan.

_____

_____

_____

_____

Name _____

Slue-Foot Sue
Vocabulary

A. Write the number of each word on the line in front of its definition.

1. proposed   _____ the edge of the settled territory

2. bustle   _____ asked to marry

3. solution   _____ a rope used to catch cattle

4. drought   _____ padding used to puff out the top of a woman's skirt at the back

5. lasso   _____ the line at which the earth and the sky seem to meet

6. constellation   _____ a group of stars that seem to form a figure or an object

7. horizon   _____ continual dry weather

8. puny   _____ feeble, weak

9. frontier   _____ the answer to a problem

B. Use the words from the list above to complete these sentences.

1. Pecos Bill _____ to Slue-Foot Sue.

2. Riding a horse while wearing a _____ is a problem.

3. Sue found a _____ to the _____ in Texas.

4. Together Bill and Sue had to _____ the Little Dipper,

     a _____.

                  Tall Tales • EMC 758

Name _____

Slue-Foot Sue
Remembering Details

A. Match the number of each description with the character it fits.

Pecos Bill   _____   _____

Slue-Foot Sue   _____   _____   _____   _____

Widow Maker   _____   _____

1. experienced catfish rider

2. ridden successfully by one rider

3. fell in love at first sight

4. wanted a store-bought outfit

5. thought of a plan to end the drought

6. powerful animal

7. anxious to be married

8. wore a bustle

B. Write sentences that describe each of the three characters above. Use all that you know to tell the most important things about the characters.

_____

_____

_____

_____

_____

 Tall Tales • EMC 758

Name _____

Slue-Foot Sue
Exaggeration

A. In tall tales things are often exaggerated. Explain the exaggeration in each sentence.

1. She was riding past his ranch on the back of a catfish.

   _____

2. Sue was blasted clean out of the saddle and into space.

   _____

3. The drought lasted so long that children didn't even know what rain was.

   _____

4. Sue told Bill to lasso the handle of the constellation.

   _____

B. Write an exaggeration about each thing below.

homework _____

_____

recess _____

_____

your desk _____

_____

Little Sir, the Rooster

Farmer Dave had a small plot of land on the coast of California. He raised vegetables, fruits, and beautiful flowers. He decided that he needed a rooster to make his farm complete. So he flipped through the pages of his farm catalog.

Within a week, the mailman brought Farmer Dave a little box. Inside was a tiny rooster with feathered feet. Farmer Dave was proud of his new rooster. He named it Little Sir. The rooster had shiny black and red feathers. The feathers on his topknot curved gracefully as he strutted around the pen.

Little Sir scratched at the gravel and flapped to his perch. "Er-tee-er-tee-ert, Er-tee-er-tee-ert!" The tiny rooster's crow echoed through the hills. As the days passed, Little Sir strutted and preened. His crow grew louder and louder.

It was soon clear that he was no ordinary rooster. Little Sir had an ear-splitting, tree-toppling crow. His crow was so loud that Farmer Dave's neighbors began to complain. Still, each day Little Sir's crow got louder. Before long the crow was so loud that Farmer Dave had to go to bed in a soundproof room. He wore earplugs to protect his hearing.

The crow continued to grow louder every day. Television crews came to record the little rooster's crow. Librarians complained. A morning noise alert was issued for the California Coast. People in Wyoming stopped setting their alarms. They listened for Little Sir's morning wake-up crow.

 Tall Tales • EMC 758

Farmer Dave didn't know what to do. He knew that he had to do something. All of his neighbors posted *For Sale* signs in their yards. He went to Little Sir's pen. He sat down beside the little rooster and talked to him. "Little Sir, I know that you're only a rooster. Most roosters don't understand humans. But I think you're special. I think that you will understand what I have to say. Your crow is too loud. Can you please do something about it?"

Little Sir tipped his head from side to side. He listened to Farmer Dave. When Dave had finished talking, Little Sir hopped up onto Farmer Dave's shoulder. He gave a tiny little crow, "Er-tee-er-tee-ert!" Then he answered Farmer Dave's question. "I will be happy to crow softly, Mr. Dave. You are a very good man. You give me greens and tomatoes every day. I love the watermelon you give me every weekend. You keep me safe from foxes and mountain lions. But you also have made a big mistake. You named me Little Sir. I have been crowing louder and louder each day hoping that you would stop calling me *little*. I may be small, but I am not little!"

Farmer Dave stared in amazement. His rooster was talking. "Little Sir, oh, ummmm, Mr. Rooster Sir, if I stop calling you little, will you stop crowing so loudly?"

"Of course," replied the rooster. "Do you have any idea how hard it is to crow so loudly?"

"Well, I'll be!" Farmer Dave smiled at the little rooster. "From now on I'm going to call you Big Sir." The little rooster strutted to the corner of the pen and gave a tiny little crow.

Farmer Dave and Big Sir still live happily on their little farm. In fact, Big Sir used his giant crow to save ships when the foghorn at the lighthouse was broken. The sailors were so grateful that they named the lighthouse after him. But that's another story for another day.

 Tall Tales • EMC 758

Name _____

Questions about
Little Sir, the Rooster

1. What is the setting of this tale?

_____

_____

2. What is the problem in the story?

_____

_____

3. Give three examples that tell the how serious the problem was.

_____

_____

_____

4. How did Farmer Dave solve the problem?

_____

_____

5. Why was the ending of the story good for the rooster and for Farmer Dave?

_____

_____

_____

Name _____

Little Sir, the Rooster
Verbs

A. Write the number of each verb from the story on the line in front of its meaning.

1. preen   _____ defend

2. strut   _____ depend upon

3. topple   _____ smooth the feathers

4. split   _____ gripe

5. count on   _____ bend

6. protect   _____ fall over

7. complain   _____ swagger, walk importantly

8. curve   _____ divide in two

B. Use the verbs above to complete these sentences.

1. The mother goose will _____ her goslings.

2. The peacock will open its tail and _____ across
   the field.

3. The animals _____ the zookeeper to feed them.

4. Farmer Dave's neighbors will _____ if he gets a
   new rooster.

Name _____

Little Sir, the Rooster
Exaggeration

A tall tale usually includes things that could happen and things that are exaggerated. **Exaggeration** is making something seem larger or better or smaller or worse than it really is.

The results of Little Sir's crowing were exaggerated in this tall tale.

List six things that probably wouldn't happen because of a rooster's crow.

_____

_____

_____

_____

_____

_____

List six things in the story that might actually happen because of a rooster's crow.

_____

_____

_____

_____

_____

_____

Name _____

Little Sir, the Rooster
A Sequel

The end of the story gives an idea for another story. Big Sir uses his giant crow to save ships when the foghorn at the lighthouse is broken. Use what you know about Farmer Dave and his rooster to write a sequel.

_____

_____

_____

_____

_____

_____

_____

_____

_____

_____

_____

_____

Stormalong—Able-Bodied Seaman

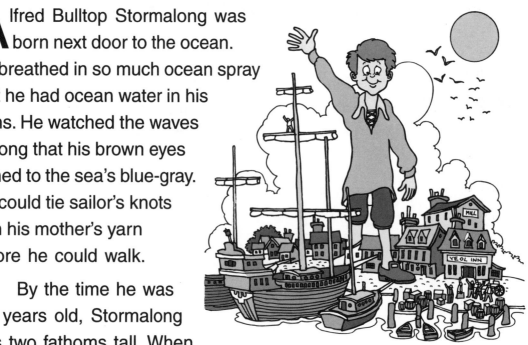

Alfred Bulltop Stormalong was born next door to the ocean. He breathed in so much ocean spray that he had ocean water in his veins. He watched the waves so long that his brown eyes turned to the sea's blue-gray. He could tie sailor's knots with his mother's yarn before he could walk.

By the time he was ten years old, Stormalong was two fathoms tall. When he was thirteen, he signed on board a schooner bound for China. Stormalong had to make a few adjustments because of his size. He couldn't stand too close to the ship's rail or the ship would list. He had to sleep in an extra-large lifeboat. A sailor's hammock wasn't long enough for him. The hardest thing he had to do was curb his appetite. Stormy could deplete the ship's supply of salt pork, jerked beef, and molasses before it even left the harbor.

On board the schooner, Stormy was happier than a sheephead in a school of sardines. Then one day the ship stopped rock-still in the ocean. The wind was blowing, the sails were full, but the ship was not moving. One of the sailors shouted, "A kraken's got hold of the keel!"

"What's a kraken?" asked Stormy.

"It's a little like an octopus, only it has more arms. It's a little like a crab, but its bite's ten times harder. Its jaws can bite a mast clean through. It can turn a ship into a pile of driftwood. It's the meanest, most vicious monster a seaman can ever meet!"

*1 Fathom = 2 yards   1 yard = 3 feet

"Men," the captain said, wringing his hands, "I need one of you to dive overboard. We need to know what's holding us back. Step forward if you would like to volunteer."

All the men except Stormalong took two steps backward. "I'd be proud to take a look, Captain," said Stormalong. The crew heaved a sigh of relief. The cook handed Stormalong a chopping cleaver, just in case. Stormalong pushed the cleaver under his belt, climbed up on the bowsprit, and dived into the water.

Below the ship's keel, Stormy saw a long clawlike arm. It was reaching up out of the blackness. The claw had hold of the ship. Then Stormy saw an eye staring up at him. If it isn't a kraken, thought Stormy, it's something worse. He pulled the cleaver from his belt and started whacking at the arm. He slashed through the arm. Two more arms sprang up and gripped the ship.

Stormalong tossed his cleaver away. He grabbed hold of one of the slippery arms. He pulled and yanked. When the arm let go of the ship, Stormy tied it in a figure-eight knot. Next he grabbed the second arm and tied it into a fisherman's bend. Stormalong wrestled each of the monster's arms. He tied them all into knots. He used knots that hadn't even been invented. Finally the monster was so tangled up, it rolled away.

Stormalong swam back to the surface. He found the schooner rocking in the towering waves caused by his underwater wrestling match. The captain was so delighted to see Stormy that he asked him to sign on then and there for the next voyage. That was the beginning of Stormalong's long and exciting career as a sailor.

Name _____

Questions about
Stormalong—Able-Bodied Seaman

1. What things about Stormalong made him a natural-born sailor?

   _____

   _____

2. If a fathom is about six feet, how tall was Stormy when he was ten?

   _____

3. What adjustments did Stormalong have to make on board the schooner?

   _____

   _____

4. How did Stormalong defeat the sea monster?

   _____

   _____

5. Do you think Stormalong was a great thinker? Tell why.

   _____

   _____

   _____

6. Sailors today sign their names by writing the initials A.B. following their name. Use story clues to tell what this means.

   _____

   _____

 Tall Tales • EMC 758

Name _____

Stormalong—Able-Bodied Seaman
Vocabulary

Write the letter of each word on the line in front of its definition. Use a dictionary if you need help.

a. schooner

b. hammock

c. lifeboat

d. sheephead

e. sardines

f. keel

g. mast

h. cleaver

i. bowsprit

j. fisherman's bend

k. list

l. jerked beef

m. salt pork

n. molasses

_____ a swinging bed

_____ dried beef

_____ a large pole to which the sails of a ship attach

_____ a knot for tying a line

_____ a boat with two masts

_____ small fish

_____ a thick brown sugar syrup

_____ a butcher's knife

_____ a boat carried by a ship for use in an emergency

_____ pork cured in salt

_____ a long pole that sticks forward from the front of a ship

_____ a fish with a large head shaped like a lamb's head

_____ the timbers along the bottom of a boat

_____ tip to one side

Name _____

Stormalong—Able-Bodied Seaman

Figures of Speech

Reread *Stormalong* to find each of the expressions listed below. Use the context to understand what they mean. Using your own words, write a simple definition of each expression.

signed on board _____

_____

happier than a sheephead in a school of sardines _____

_____

stopped rock-still _____

_____

clean through _____

_____

then and there _____

_____

Name _____

Stormalong—Able-bodied Seaman
Cause and Effect

Write what happens in the story as a result of each of these actions.

1. Stormalong stood next to the rail of the ship.

_____

_____

2. Stormalong breathed in a lot of ocean spray.

_____

_____

3. Stormalong watched the sea's waves all the time.

_____

_____

4. Stormalong and the monster wrestled underwater.

_____

_____

5. Stormalong tied the monster's arms into knots.

_____

_____

Paul Bunyan

Paul Bunyan was born on a very special day—July 4th. Paul Bunyan was a very special baby. He was the biggest, strongest baby ever born in the state of Maine. He weighed just a little over 156 pounds. He could walk from that very first day. Just like many toddlers, Paul got himself into more than his share of trouble.

Now Paul's father was in the logging business. Paul, like many little boys, liked to help his dad. He walked about pickin' up trees by their roots and settin' them in his father's lumber wagon. This was mighty distressing to the Bunyans' neighbors. They didn't like having their trees plucked by a large baby. But Paul didn't mean any harm. He was just tryin' to help.

Paul's parents tried to calm down their neighbors. They took his cradle out into the harbor and anchored it there. At first, Paul thought it was fun to watch the gulls glide and dip. Then he got bored. There was nothin' to do. So Paul took to rockin' his cradle back and forth. As he rocked, the waves in the harbor started gettin' bigger and bigger. Before long the entire town was flooded by the waves.

The Bunyans decided to move into the backwoods where Paul could play without doin' too much harm. Paul loved livin' in the wilderness. He raced with the deer and wrestled with the grizzlies. Paul grew to be a very strong young man.

Tall Tales • EMC 758

One strange winter after a blizzard of blue snow, Paul found a new friend. He was walkin' about doin' his morning chores. He heard a soft moan comin' from one of the blue snowdrifts. He plowed through the snow to the drift and began diggin'. There was a baby ox the same blue color as the snow. Paul rescued that baby and took it home as his pet. He named the ox Babe.

Every morning after that, Paul would pick Babe up and give him a big hug. Now Babe continued to grow at an amazing rate. Soon he was as big as a small building. Paul still picked him up and gave him a hug every morning. Babe grew bigger and heavier. Paul continued givin' him a morning hug. Some people believe Paul gained his great strength because of this morning ox-lifting exercise.

When Paul was seventeen, he decided that it was time to leave home and make a life of his own. He and Babe began an adventure that would take them across the whole United States. Together they cleared forests to make way for the building of America.

Tall Tales • EMC 758

Name _____

Questions about
Paul Bunyan

1. What was special about Paul Bunyan's birthday?

_____

_____

2. Why were the Bunyans' neighbors distressed?

_____

_____

3. How did Paul's parents solve this problem? Was their solution successful?

_____

_____

_____

4. How did Paul fill his days in the backwoods?

_____

_____

5. What helped Paul Bunyan grow so strong?

_____

_____

6. Why did Paul leave home?

_____

_____

48

Name _____

Paul Bunyan
Vocabulary

Read the sentences. Complete the statements about the underlined words.
Then write your own sentences using the words correctly.

1. Just like many <u>toddlers</u>, Paul got himself into more than his share of trouble.

    a. In this sentence, <u>toddler</u> means "a child just learning to walk."   yes   no

    b. _____

    _____

2. This was mighty <u>distressing</u> to the Bunyans' neighbors.

    a. In this sentence, <u>distressing</u> means "upsetting."   yes   no

    b. _____

    _____

3. Paul's parents <u>anchored</u> his cradle out in the harbor.

    a. In this sentence, <u>anchored</u> means "provided with food and water."   yes   no

    b. _____

    _____

4. Paul <u>wrestled</u> with grizzlies and grew to be a very strong young man.

    a. In this sentence, <u>wrestled</u> means "to struggle with a problem."   yes   no

    b. _____

    _____

        Tall Tales • EMC 758

Name _____

Paul Bunyan

A Comparison

Compare Paul Bunyan's childhood with your childhood.

	Paul Bunyan	_____ (your name)
Birthday		
Birth Weight		
Father's Occupation		
Favorite Things To Do		
Pets		

Tall Tales • EMC 758

Name _____

Paul Bunyan

A Time Line

This tall tale tells a little about Paul Bunyan's first seventeen years. Write one important event in each box. Start at the bottom when Paul was a baby. Keep the events in chronological order.

Babe, the Blue Ox

Paul Bunyan's blue ox, Babe, was enormous. The lumberjacks could line up fifty-four axes end to end between his eyes. His horns were like two huge, pointed drills. If he flicked a fly off his hindquarters, the swish of his great tail would start a wind. That wind blew hats off heads two miles away.

It was hard finding enough food for Babe. He ate so much hay that it took twenty wagons to deliver enough for one day. Fields of carrots and turnips were only tiny, tasty treats. Keeping Babe from getting thirsty was another problem entirely.

During one dry, hot September, Paul and Babe were traveling across the sagebrush country of eastern Washington. They had gone six days and six nights without having a drop of water to drink. Paul and his men were thirsty. But Babe the Blue Ox was the thirstiest of all.

On the seventh day they came upon a deep canyon with towering cliffs on either side. Down that deep canyon surged a mighty river. Its sandbars shone in the sunlight. Swirling water swept downstream over a thundering waterfall.

Well, when Babe spotted that water, you can imagine what happened! The thirsty ox began to drink! He stood knee-deep in the center of the river and buried his nose in the cool water. He drank and drank. He never even stopped for a breath. After his first few gulps, the water in the river dropped ten feet. The shoreline began to change. Babe was drinking the river dry!

Great schools of fish were caught on the sandbars. The roaring falls dried up to a thin trickle. Two men who were crossing the river in a canoe were left stranded on the river bottom. They looked pretty silly trying to paddle their canoe on dry land.

Babe gave a bellow of delight that could be heard in New York City. He was feeling good. He had quenched his great thirst. He didn't realize that he had caused a whole river to disappear from the face of the earth. Yet that's exactly what happened. The river never flowed again.

Today there are only a few stagnant pools of water where the river used to be. A sign says "The Lost River of Grand Coulee." People scratch their heads and puzzle over the origin of the name. If they heard this story of Paul Bunyan and Babe, his blue ox, they might understand.

     Tall Tales • EMC 758

Name _____

Questions about
Babe, the Blue Ox

1. What two things make Babe an appropriate tall tale character?

   _____   _____

2. What problem did Babe have in this tale?

   _____

3. How was Babe's problem solved? What happened as a result?

   _____

   _____

4. Tell whether the following story facts could be true. Justify your answers.

   a. Babe was so big that fifty-four axes could be lined up end   true   false
      to end between his eyes.

      _____

   b. Swirling water swept downstream over a thundering waterfall.   true   false

      _____

   c. Babe drank the river dry.   true   false

      _____

   d. Babe gave a bellow that could be heard in New York City.   true   false

      _____

Name _____

Babe, the Blue Ox
Vocabulary

A. Draw a line between the two words combined in each of these compound words. Then write the number of each word on the line in front of its definition.

1. downstream   _____ a bank of sand at the mouth of a harbor

2. sandbar   _____ the line formed by the meeting of the shore and water

3. sagebrush   _____ light from the sun

4. hindquarters   _____ a plant native to the dry plains

5. sunlight   _____ the back end of a four-legged animal

6. knee-deep   _____ a sufficient depth to cover a person up to the knees

7. shoreline   _____ in the direction in which a stream or river flows

B. Use the compound words above to complete these sentences.

1. The raft was moving _____.

2. Then it went aground on a _____.

3. The people on the _____ called for help.

4. The wheat in the field was _____.

5. Only _____ grew on the dry land.

            Tall Tales • EMC 758

Name _____

Babe, the Blue Ox
Alphabetical Order

Number each set of words in alphabetical order.

_____ flicked

_____ finding

_____ fifty

_____ falls

_____ few

_____ feeling

_____ river

_____ reptile

_____ realize

_____ riverbed

_____ really

_____ recent

_____ shone

_____ sagebrush

_____ silly

_____ sandbars

_____ shoreline

_____ sunlight

_____ treats

_____ thin

_____ tail

_____ thirsty

_____ tiny

_____ tasty

Name _____

Babe, the Blue Ox
Understanding Word Meanings

Answer these questions using complete sentences.

1. What is something you might puzzle over?

_____

_____

2. What might travel in a school?

_____

_____

3. Why would you give a bellow of delight?

_____

_____

4. What would you consider a tiny, tasty treat?

_____

_____

5. How would you quench your thirst?

_____

_____

6. What is the place of your origin?

_____

_____

Paul Bunyan Digs Puget Sound

One spring Babe the Blue Ox became sick. Paul decided the only way to save his companion was to move west. He would nurse Babe with whales' milk. After the long journey, Babe was very weak. Paul was so discouraged that he began digging a grave. Amazingly, the ox suddenly got better. Paul couldn't think of what to do with the big hole he'd started to dig. Then he met Peter Puget.

Mr. Puget suggested that Paul finish digging the hole. The hole could be a new harbor for Seattle. Seattle's harbor wasn't big enough to float a rowboat. Mr. Puget and his crew had worked for a whole summer. They hadn't moved enough dirt to fill a good-sized sandbox. Paul liked the idea. He and Babe would dredge a sound that would be the talk of the country. The sound would have room for one hundred boats. Paul figured that the sound would help him float his logs to the mill. "We'll call it Puget Sound, since you're the man with the idea," he told Mr. Puget.

The people who lived around Seattle and Tacoma felt that Paul's plan was impossible. They watched as Paul hitched a giant scoop shovel to Babe, and the two started to work. Paul and Babe scraped and shoveled. They filled the scoop shovel over and over. No one wanted the dirt dumped on the shore, so Paul hauled it way back into the mountains. When the sound was completed, the piles of dirt were so high they could be seen for miles. The people named them Mount Rainier and Mount Baker.

All the people in the area wanted the sound to run in different directions. The folks by Tacoma wanted it to go in their direction. Someone near Everett wanted a harbor there. Paul worked hard trying to keep everybody happy. That's the reason that the sound has so many turns and twists. When he was almost through, he remembered another promise he had made. So he scooped out Hood Canal to the west.

Paul had a party to celebrate the completion of the project. A few people near Whidbey Peninsula refused to come. They wanted the sound to be named Whidbey Sound. They even had maps printed with the name in big letters.

Well, Paul didn't like the idea. He was so upset he decided to fill the sound back up. He took his shovel and threw shovel after shovel of dirt into the channel. The dirt made a thousand little islands dotting the sound. Then Paul took his pickax and cut a narrow passage across the Whidbey Peninsula. Whidbey Peninsula became an island.

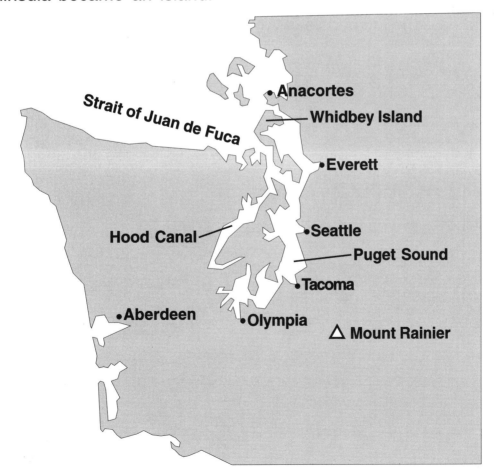

Name _____

Questions about
Paul Bunyan Digs Puget Sound

1. Why did Paul Bunyan take Babe to Washington State?

_____

_____

2. How did Puget Sound come to be?

_____

_____

3. How does the story explain the formation of Mount Rainier and Mount Baker?

_____

_____

4. How would you describe the people of Whidbey Peninsula?

_____

_____

5. Which phrase describes Paul Bunyan's motives as he dug the sound?

   ○ Paul wanted fame and fortune for himself.

   ○ Paul wanted to please all of the people.

   ○ Paul wanted to punish the people of Whidbey Peninsula.

   ○ Paul wanted to create a memorial for Babe.

Name _____

Paul Bunyan Digs Puget Sound
Vocabulary

A. Some words have several different meanings. In this tale *some* words have special meanings relating to the sea. Write the number of the meaning that matches each word. Some words will have more than one meaning.

sound _____ _____   peninsula _____

canal _____ _____   mainland _____

harbor _____ _____   passage _____

1. a tubular passage in the body, as in the ear, for example

2. to keep in your mind

3. a way through

4. a channel for water cut through land

5. vibrations that travel through the air

6. a large body of land, not including nearby islands

7. a piece of land that is almost surrounded by water

8. an arm of the sea

9. a place of shelter for ships

B. Use the words above to complete these sentences.

1. The Puget _____ is located off the coast of Washington.

2. It provides a safe _____ for ships.

3. You will need a boat to get from the _____ to the island.

Name _____

Paul Bunyan Digs Puget Sound
Find It on the Map

Circle the names of places in the story.

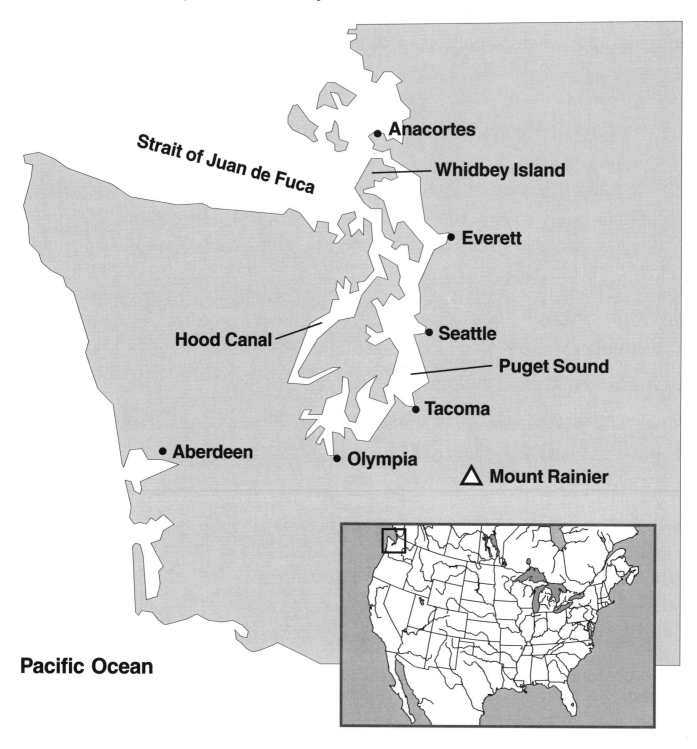

Anacortes

Whidbey Island

Strait of Juan de Fuca

Everett

Hood Canal

Seattle

Puget Sound

Tacoma

Aberdeen

Olympia

△ Mount Rainier

Pacific Ocean

Name _____

Paul Bunyan Digs Puget Sound
How Did It Happen?

Many tall tales give fanciful explanations for geographic features such as mountains, canyons, and lakes. Tell the reason the story gives for each of these features.

1. Puget Sound

_____

_____

2. Mount Rainier

_____

_____

3. Hood Canal

_____

_____

4. the islands in Puget Sound

_____

_____

5. the narrow passage between the mainland and Whidbey Island

_____

_____

Pea Soup Shorty

Paul Bunyan had to feed a lot of hungry lumberjacks. He was looking for a good cook who might be able to help. One day a new man came into camp. His name was Pea Soup Shorty. He always had a big kettle of pea soup simmering on the stove. No matter how many sat down to eat, there was always enough pea soup to go around.

The men liked his pea soup. The first season Shorty used up all the peas in that part of the country. Shorty was heartbroken. He couldn't make his famous pea soup. He tried using BB shot painted green, but that didn't work out so well. The men ate the soup, but they got so heavy they couldn't do their work.

Then Shorty heard of a farmer on the other side of the country who had a bumper crop of peas. He hitched Babe the Blue Ox to a big wagon and went to pick up the peas. He didn't have any trouble until he was driving back. His wagon was loaded with eight tons of peas. As they were going along Bubbling Springs Lake, a wheel got stuck. The wagon tipped over. All the peas rolled into the lake.

Pea Soup Shorty sat by the lake and rubbed his head. He watched as the lake turned green. It was a shame to waste all those peas. And now, what was he going to feed the men? He turned around to go. His hat slipped from his hand and tumbled into the water. Shorty reached for it and pulled his hand back fast. The water in Bubbling Springs Lake was hot! He licked his fingers. Ummm!— pea soup!

 Tall Tales • EMC 758

The whole lake was like a great hot kettle of pea soup! The little cook's eyes twinkled. He could feed all the men with fresh pea soup and have plenty left over. He hurried back to camp and loaded a huge pot onto the wagon. Babe pulled the wagon back and forth from the lake. The men had all the nice, hot pea soup they could eat.

When Paul saw the pea soup lake, he hired an old sternwheeler to help Shorty with the stirring. Pea Soup Shorty became famous for his never-ending supply of delicious pea soup.

"Using the lake was my idea," Shorty bragged. "I just decided to dump the wagon load of peas into the lake. Nobody else would ever have thought of that!"

Babe just winked one huge eye and snorted softly to himself.

 Tall Tales • EMC 758

Name _____

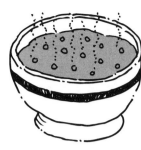

Questions about
Pea Soup Shorty

1. How do you think Paul Bunyan's cook got his name?

_____

_____

2. What happened that caused a problem for the cook?

_____

_____

3. What was the cook's first solution to the problem? Was it successful?

_____

_____

_____

4. What was the cook's second solution to the problem? Was it successful?

_____

_____

_____

5. Why did Babe wink one huge eye when the cook boasted, "Using the lake was my idea"?

_____

_____

66

Name _____

Pea Soup Shorty
Vocabulary

A. Write the number of each word on the line in front of its definition.

1. ton

_____ a steamboat propelled by a large paddle wheel

2. sternwheeler

_____ kept close to a boiling point

3. BB

_____ two thousand pounds

4. simmering

_____ constant

5. lumberjack

_____ a small lead pellet for firing from a gun

6. never-ending

_____ a person who cuts timber

B. Explain what the underlined words and phrases in these sentences mean.

1. Pea Soup Shorty was <u>heartbroken</u>.

_____

2. The farmer had a <u>bumper crop</u> of peas.

_____

3. There was <u>always enough to go around</u>.

_____

Name _____

Pea Soup Shorty
Sequencing Story Events

Number the events in the order in which they occurred in the story.

_____ Babe winked.

_____ The wagon tipped over.

_____ Shorty was heartbroken.

_____ Shorty used up all the peas.

_____ Shorty used BBs painted green.

_____ The peas rolled into the lake.

_____ The sternwheeler stirred the soup.

On another sheet of paper, draw a picture of your favorite part of the story.

 Tall Tales • EMC 758

Name _____

Pea Soup Shorty
Cause and Effect

Write the cause of each event.

1. Paul Bunyan hired Pea Soup Shorty.

_____

_____

2. Pea Soup Shorty used up all the peas.

_____

_____

3. The men were so heavy they couldn't do their work.

_____

_____

4. The hot water in Bubbling Springs Lake turned green.

_____

_____

5. Pea Soup Shorty became famous.

_____

_____

69   Tall Tales • EMC 758

John Henry—A Steel-Drivin' Man

Folks say that John Henry was born with a hammer in his hand. Baby John Henry would crawl around his parents' cabin bangin' on the wood floor with his daddy's hammer. 'Tweren't many years before John Henry was a big, strong man with a hammer of his own.

John Henry was a hard worker and he tried lots of different jobs. He plowed fields and picked cotton. He poled a Mississippi barge all the way from Minnesota to New Orleans. But nothin' pleased John Henry more than the feel of a hammer in his hand.

Now this was the time when it seemed like all the folks in the country were movin' west. And, you know, where people go, the railroad goes too. Well, thousands of miles of track had to be laid. And that was just the job for John Henry. With his hammer swingin' twelve hours a day, John Henry and his crew pushed the railroad west.

One day John Henry and his crew reached the foot of a mammoth mountain. "Men," exclaimed John Henry, "the tracks can't go on if we don't tunnel through this here mountain." Now tunnelin' through a mountain is hard, dangerous work, but John Henry liked a challenge. The men began to drill, inch by inch, through the solid rock of the mountain.

A week later a huge machine appeared near the tunnel entrance. The man in the driver's seat started in braggin' to John Henry's crew. "This here steam drill can out-work seven men!"

Now this got John Henry's dander up. He stepped in front of the drill and hollered up to the driver, "There ain't no machine ever been made that I can't out-drill!"

So the contest began—man against machine. John Henry worked on one side of the mountain. The machine worked on the other side of the mountain. For days the drilling went on. Neither man nor machine rested. John Henry kept on swingin' night and day. He held a sledgehammer in each hand. The drill he was poundin' on got so hot that it showed fiery red. The steam drill puffed and ground. Then the steam drill started to make a loud clink-clanking sound. The machine moved slower and slower, until finally it stopped runnin'. It was as still as a statue.

As tired as he was, John Henry kept on swingin' his hammers. Suddenly, with a loud cracking sound, the last pieces of granite fell away. John Henry broke through! He looked up with a smile that said, "I told you so." Then he fell to the ground dead. His heart was plumb worn out, but the hammers were still in his hands.

Name _____

Questions about *John Henry—*
A Steel-Drivin' Man

1. What kind of work did John Henry like best?

   _____

   _____

2. What were some of the other jobs that John Henry tried?

   _____

   _____

3. Why did John Henry challenge the steam drill to a contest?

   _____

   _____

4. What was happening in the United States when men like John Henry were building the railroad?

   _____

   _____

5. Who won the contest? Why?

   _____

   _____

6. Why does the storyteller end the tale with "but the hammers were still in his hands"?

   _____

   _____

Name _____

John Henry—A Steel-Drivin' Man
Vocabulary

A. Match each word with its meaning.

exclaimed	boasted
bragged	cried out with surprise
hollered	made a long, deep sound of pain
groaned	shouted

B. Use the best word from the list above to complete each of these sentences.

The roller blader _____ that he could do every trick.

The crowd _____ as he completed the first pass.

The bystander _____ a warning.

He _____ as he tried to stand after his fall.

C. Match each phrase with its definition.

got his dander up	made a start
plumb worn out	exhausted
'tweren't	it wasn't
set out	made him angry

Name _____

John Henry—A Steel-Drivin' Man
Nouns and Verbs

Tell whether the underlined word in each sentence is used as a noun or a verb. Then write the correct meaning from the Word Box for each underlined word.

| ground | 1. He planted the seeds in the ground. | _____ |

meaning _____

2. The machine ground the coffee beans. _____

meaning _____

| drill | 3. The bit will drill a hole in the wood. | _____ |

meaning _____

4. Have you ever used a drill? _____

meaning _____

| hammer | 5. The hammer is an important tool. | _____ |

meaning _____

6. Dad will hammer the peg into the wall. _____

meaning _____

Word Box		
crushed	strike loudly	a tool with a heavy metal head
make a hole	soil or earth	a pointed tool used for boring holes

         Tall Tales • EMC 758

Name _____

John Henry—A Steel-Drivin' Man
Alliteration

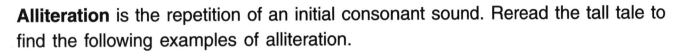

Alliteration is the repetition of an initial consonant sound. Reread the tall tale to find the following examples of alliteration.

Henry...hammer....hand

plowed...picked...poled

clink-clanking

For each of the words below, write several adjectives that begin with the same consonant letter. Then use two adjectives to write a phrase describing each object.

hammer _____

_____

drill _____

_____

track _____

_____

mountain _____

_____

statue _____

_____

Joe Magarac—Steelman of Pittsburgh

When the steel mills around Pittsburgh are fired up, the sky burns with their fires. People say, "Joe Magarac must be back on the job." It was a long time ago that Joe Magarac, the greatest steelworker that ever lived, came to Pittsburgh.

The first time that anyone ever saw Joe was at Big Steve's contest. Steve Mestrovich, the steel boss, invited everyone in Allegheny County to a contest. His daughter, Mary, was ready to marry. Big Steve was determined that she would marry the strongest steelman.

Big Steve and Mary stood on a platform in the center of a field. Steve pointed to three iron bars in front of the platform. "I have iron bars here. The first bar is for beginners. It weighs only three hundred pounds. The second bar weighs five hundred pounds. The third will help me choose a man for Mary. It weighs as much as the other two together. Let's get started."

The young men pulled off their shirts and stepped over to the iron bars. Pete Pussick, Mary's favorite, smiled as he leaned down. He lifted the first bar without a grunt. Others followed. Some were successful and some weren't. "I'm the best man for you," Pete whispered in Mary's ear. She handed him a geranium blossom.

Pete stepped over to the second bar. He set his muscles, gritted his teeth, and lifted it. Others followed. A few were successful. Many were not. Everyone knew that Mary hoped that Pete Pussick would be declared the winner.

The crowd was silent. Pete bent over the third bar. He spit on his hands and spread his feet wide. He stooped down and grabbed the bar. He pulled and strained. His face was as red as Mary's silk dress. Pete could not lift the bar. He gave up and stood with his head down. All the other men took a turn. No one could lift the bar.

Tall Tales • EMC 758

Then out of the crowd came a booming laugh. A big black-haired man appeared. His back was as broad as an ore car from the mines. His wrists were as big around as shiny steel drums. He was munching on two paprika chickens and laughing between the bites. He walked forward. He picked up the heavy iron bar in one hand and Pete Pussick in the other.

The stranger put Pete on the ground gently. He twisted the iron bar into a figure eight and tossed it aside. He introduced himself as Joe Magarac. The men laughed at first because "magarac" in Hungarian means jackass. But Joe only shrugged. He was like a jackass—all he did was eat and work. He pulled off his shirt and showed the crowd his chest. It shone like polished steel. When Big Steve rapped his knuckles against Joe's ribs, there was a sound like ringing metal.

Joe was a steelman—steel from head to toe. Big Steve pulled Mary over to Joe and said, "I've found you the strongest husband." Mary looked at Joe Magarac and then she looked back longingly at Pete Pussick.

Joe looked at Mary. "You're a pretty girl. Your eyes are as blue as blooming cornflowers. Your hair is like the golden sunlight in the fields. You'll be a fine wife for somebody. But me? I have no time for a wife. I only have time to work and to eat. Why don't you marry that man over there? He's the strongest here, next to me." Joe nodded toward Pete.

So the wedding took place. Mary married Pete Pussick. Joe enjoyed the wedding feast. For six hours he ate noodles, fat and spicy sausages, and brown loaves of bread. Then he walked back to the steel mills.

Name _____

Questions about *Joe Magarac—*
Steelman of Pittsburgh

1. What do the steelworkers of Pittsburgh remember about Joe Magarac?

_____

_____

2. What does **magarac** mean in Hungarian? Tell why that was a good name for Joe.

_____

_____

3. Do you think Mary had made her choice for a husband before the contest began? Tell why you think as you do.

_____

_____

_____

4. In most tall tales the main character is the winner. What makes *Joe Magarac* different?

_____

_____

5. How was Joe like a machine?

_____

_____

_____

Name _____

Joe Magarac—
Steelman of Pittsburgh

Sequencing Story Events

Number the events in the order they occurred in the story.

_____ Joe twisted the bar into a figure eight.

_____ Pete Pussick whispered in Mary's ear.

_____ The steel boss invited everyone to his contest.

_____ Mary gave Pete a geranium blossom.

_____ Joe appeared in the crowd.

_____ Big Steve said that he'd found a strong man for Mary.

_____ The crowd laughed at Joe's name.

_____ Joe picked up the heaviest bar.

_____ Joe refused to marry Mary.

_____ After six hours of eating, Joe walked back to the steel mill.

Name _____

Joe Magarac—
Steelman of Pittsburgh
Similes and Metaphors

A **simile** is a figure of speech that makes a comparison using the words **like** or **as**
A **metaphor** also makes comparisons, but without using the words **like** or **as**.

simile—The frost decorated the fence **like a lacy curtain**.

metaphor—My garden was quiet under **its blanket of snow**.

A. Tell the two things that are being compared. Then circle the correct label.

1. The sky burns.

_____ _____   simile   metaphor

2. His face was as red as Mary's silk dress.

_____ _____   simile   metaphor

3. His back was as broad as an ore car from the mines.

_____ _____   simile   metaphor

4. His wrists were as big around as shiny steel drums.

_____ _____   simile   metaphor

5. It glittered like polished steel.

_____ _____   simile   metaphor

B. On another sheet of paper, write a simile of your own about something in the story.

                           Tall Tales • EMC 758

Name _____

Joe Magarac—
Steelman of Pittsburgh
More Than One Meaning

Words often have more than one meaning. The words below have a common meaning and a second meaning related to making steel. Find the two meanings for each word and write the numbers on the lines. Then circle the number that has something to do with making steel.

pit	_____	_____
bar	_____	_____
mill	_____	_____
drums	_____	_____
car	_____	_____
fired up	_____	_____

1. a hole in the ground from which ore is dug

2. a place where refreshments are served

3. a percussion instrument

4. having been set on fire

5. an automobile

6. a cart with wheels that follows a track as it hauls ore out of a mine

7. excited

8. the stone of a fruit

9. cylindrical containers

10. machinery for grinding grain

11. a long piece of steel

12. a building fitted with machinery for processing iron ore

Mike Fink

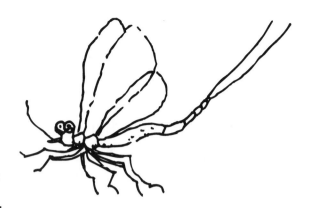

Mike Fink grew up in the woods around Pittsburgh. He practiced bragging as he whooped and hollered through the woods. He claimed to be half wild horse, half alligator, and half snapping turtle. Mike practiced shooting too. He shot at wolves, bobcats, skunks, and mosquitoes.

He was still in knee pants when he decided to enter a shooting contest. The other men in the contest smiled behind their hands. They made fun of young Mike. One even offered to lift him up so he could see the target. But Mike wasn't put off. He didn't let the older men scare him. What's more, he was as good at shooting off his mouth as he was at shooting a gun. He told the men that he could shoot a bug faster than it could sting. To prove his point, he gave a loud whoop. He jumped into the air, kicked up his heels, and shot a passing mosquito. The mosquito flipped over and landed at Mike's feet. Mike bent down and tickled its tummy with a tuft of grass. The mosquito blinked an eye and buzzed off.

"You didn't kill that mosquito!" one man laughed.

"Nope," said Mike. "Didn't say I'd kill it. Just shot off its stinger so it wouldn't be no bother during the contest."

After that, the contest started. All the men took turns stepping up to a line that was drawn in the dirt. They each took careful aim. No one hit the bull's-eye on the target. Finally it was Mike's turn. He stepped forward. With an ear-splitting whoop he pulled the trigger. The bullet zipped right through the bull's-eye.

Tall Tales • EMC 758

The crowd clapped. "I'll bet you can't do that again, sonny," challenged one of the other shooters.

"Well, sir, I paid for five shots. I aim to drive the other four right on top of that first one," Mike boasted. And that's just what he did. He hit the bull's-eye five times in a row. Someone suggested that the other marksmen give up shooting and take up knitting instead.

When Mike was seventeen, he decided he wanted to learn a trade. He watched the men who ran the boats near the docks. They were strong and powerful. Most of them were as full of brag as he was. He told his folks farewell and packed up his gun. He headed for the first keelboat he saw.

Mike's bluster and bluff paid off. He went on to become a famous keelboat captain. In fact, he was so famous that he was known as the King of the River. One man on each keelboat wore a red feather in his cap to let others know that he was the strongest and toughest. Well, Mike's hat had so many feathers that it looked like a campfire. You could hear him bellow ten miles away. "I can out-run, out-shoot, out-fight, and out-brag anyone on this here river!"

Tall Tales • EMC 758

Name _____

Questions about *Mike Fink*

1. Which words tell about Mike Fink? Give an example from the
   story that supports your opinion.

   a good shot   yes   no

   _____

   _____

   soft-spoken and humble   yes   no

   _____

   _____

   strong and determined   yes   no

   _____

   _____

2. What did Mike do to the mosquito?

   _____

   _____

3. Why did Mike Fink decide to become a river boatman?

   _____

   _____

4. A tag line is an explanation that sometimes follows the title of a story. Which tag
   line is best for this tale?

   ○ King of the Frontier   ○ Mighty Marksman   ○ Riverboat Captain

Name _____

Mike Fink
Vocabulary

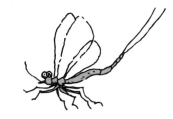

A. Match the synonyms.

braggin'   hollerin'

leapin'   jumpin'

whoopin'   boastin'

B. Some words are used to talk about certain subjects. **Quarterback** and **touchdown** are words usually used to talk about **football**. Write the words in the Word Box in the correct columns.

riverboat words   shooting words

_____   _____

_____   _____

_____   _____

_____   _____

Word Box		
keelboat	poling it up and down	captain
bull's-eye	target	aim
marksman	docks	

Name _____

Mike Fink
Special Meanings

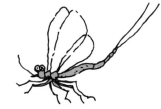

Mark the word or words that have the same meaning as the underlined phrases.

1. Mike wasn't <u>put off</u>.

   ○ removed from   ○ stopped   ○ upset

2. The other men <u>smiled behind their hands</u>.

   ○ didn't want to show their teeth   ○ told jokes
   ○ doubted Mike could win the contest

3. I shot off its stinger so it <u>wouldn't be no bother</u> during the contest.

   ○ wouldn't annoy me   ○ wouldn't sting   ○ would die

4. Most of the river boatmen <u>were full of brag</u>.

   ○ ate lots of sausage   ○ boasted about their strength
   ○ were rich

5. Mike's <u>bluster and bluff</u> paid off.

   ○ book learning   ○ a storm on a cliff   ○ bragging

6. Use one of the underlined phrases above to write a sentence that tells about Mike Fink.

   _____

   _____

                                       Tall Tales • EMC 758

Name _____

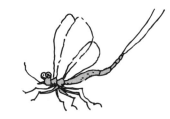

Mike Fink
Origins of Tall Tales

Some tall tales began with real people and real events. Read this article about the man that was the real Mike Fink. Compare the facts with the tall tale.

> Mike Fink was born at Fort Pitt (today the town is named Pittsburgh) in 1770. As a young man he was an expert marksman and an Indian scout. At sixteen he won a shooting contest. Each entrant had five chances to hit a bull's-eye. Mike hit the bull's-eye on the first try, but his other shots left no marks on the target. When the judge examined the target, he found that all five of Mike's bullets had passed through the same hole.
>
> In the early 1800s, before the steamboat was invented, most shipping was done by keelboat—flat-bottomed boats that could carry more than sixty tons of cargo on their decks. Mike Fink worked on keelboats along the Ohio and Mississippi Rivers. He was captain of his own boat, the Lightfoot.
>
> When steamboats took over the river trade, Mike Fink decided to become a trapper. He was killed in 1823 on his first expedition. Stories differ about how he died, but his death seems to have been the result of a quarrel during a shooting match.

Similarities	Differences
_____	_____
_____	_____
_____	_____
_____	_____

Sal Fink

The Mississippi River boatman Mike Fink had one daughter named Sal. Sal was known up and down the Mississippi as "The Screamer." Whenever she felt the urge, she let out a whoop that could be heard from Minneapolis to New Orleans. Folks told about the time she fought a duel with a thunderbolt. They remembered how she sang "Yankee Doodle" while ridin' down the river on the back of an alligator.

Sal grew up in a cabin in Kentucky with her ma and pa. She had grit as well as looks. One day she was out in the forest huntin' wildcats. She intended to use the skins for winter bedding. Suddenly she was ambushed by a band of riverboat pirates. She was like a wild mother bear. She clawed and cracked the pirates. But there were too many scoundrels in the band. The pirates worked together to hog-tie Sal. They carried her to Dead Man's Hollow, where they tied her to a tree. Then they argued about what they should do with her.

A few of the men wanted to kill her on the spot. One group thought they should hold her for ransom. Still another group wanted to sell her to the Indians. Well, the pirates argued and fussed while Sal bided her time. The pirates built a warm fire and decided to sleep on their decision.

88

The pirates finally dropped off to sleep. Sal burst the ropes that held her like they were worn laces on an old shoe. She stood with her hands on her hips and looked at the sleeping pirates. She was figurin' in her head the best way to deal with the scurvy lot. She tied the men's feet together and wound a long rope around all their feet. The sleeping pirates were connected like bananas in a bunch.

Sal let out one of her famous screams and pulled on the rope. The pirates found themselves feet-first in the burning embers of their own fire. The pirates struggled to undo themselves. Sal grabbed a pile of wildcat pelts and a chest of gold. She was off faster than a racehorse heading for the barn.

When she got home, she hauled the pelts into the house and settled in for a quick nap. She confided to her ma, "Fightin' pirates ain't very relaxin'. After all, a lady has to have her beauty rest."

         Tall Tales • EMC 758

Name _____

Questions about
Sal Fink

1. What is the setting of this tale?

_____

_____

2. Why was Sal in the forest?

_____

_____

3. The tale says that Sal was ambushed by a band of riverboat pirates. What is the best synonym for the word **ambushed** in this sentence?

○ befriended   ○ attacked   ○ visited

4. Why were the pirates able to tie Sal to the tree?

_____

_____

5. How would you describe Sal?

   ○ a shy, delicate girl
   ○ a hard-working student
   ○ a fearless frontierswoman

6. Why did Sal get the nickname "The Screamer"?

_____

_____

Name _____

Sal Fink

Understanding Expressions

Write a word or phrase that explains the underlined words in each sentence.
Then rewrite each sentence using your definition in place of the underlined words.

1. Sal let out a whoop whenever she <u>felt the urge</u>.

   felt the urge means _____

   _____

2. She <u>had grit</u> as well as looks.

   had grit means _____

   _____

3. The pirates <u>hog-tied</u> Sal.

   hog-tied means _____

   _____

4. Sal <u>bided her time</u> while the pirates argued.

   bided her time means _____

   _____

5. A lady has to have her <u>beauty rest</u>.

   beauty rest means _____

   _____

Name _____

Sal Fink

Sequencing Story Events

Number the events in the order in which they occurred in the story.

_____ Sal settled in for her beauty rest.

_____ Sal burst the ropes that held her.

_____ Sal let out one of her famous screams.

_____ Sal went into the forest to hunt wildcats.

_____ The pirates argued about what they would do with Sal.

_____ Sal grabbed a pile of pelts and a chest of gold.

_____ Sal tied the men's feet together.

_____ Sal was captured by a band of pirates.

Tall Tales • EMC 758

Name _____

Sal Fink
Using Similes

A **simile** is a comparison that helps readers form a picture in their minds.
Write the two things being compared in each of these similes from *Sal Fink.* Then draw a picture to show how you see the action described.

Sal was like a wild mother bear. She clawed and cracked the pirates. _____ _____	The sleeping pirates were connected like bananas in a bunch. _____ _____

Johnny Appleseed

If you're ever in the Ohio Valley in the early morning, stop to look. You may see smoke rising from the apple orchards along the rivers. Don't worry about that smoke. It's only Johnny Appleseed heating his morning coffee on his campfire. Soon he will stand and move through the trees. He wears his tin pot on his head. His shirt is made from a flour sack. His feet are often bare. His traveling companions? Well, the animals of the forests are his best friends. The wolf cub he rescued long ago is always by his side. Johnny Appleseed has been traveling through these same forests since the early 1800s.

You see, Johnny Appleseed was an apple missionary. He spread apples all over the frontier. He carried deerskin sacks of dried apple seeds to the wilderness. He paddled his canoe along the streams that branched off the Ohio River. He called to settlers to take his seeds and sow them. The settlers asked Johnny for advice on planting the seeds.

But Johnny wasn't satisfied with his canoe work. He wanted to reach the areas of the wilderness beyond the riverbanks. Johnny left his canoe, slung a bag of seeds over his shoulder, and started off across the new country. He planted many of the seeds himself. Whenever he came upon a sunny clearing, he dug holes with his stick. He gently placed the tiny seeds into the moist brown earth.

The wilderness was filled with wild animals—bears, wolves, wild hogs, and snakes. Johnny loved the animals. He never hurt a living thing. He sang for them as he walked through the woods. He read them stories from his Bible each night by firelight. People told stories of seeing Johnny wrestling with bear cubs while the mother bear looked on unconcerned.

Whenever Johnny did meet settlers, he gave them apple seeds. He talked with them about pies and jams and cobblers and salads. Johnny Appleseed watched the new country grow up around him. He was known in every Native American village and log cabin from Ohio to Lake Michigan. The Shawnee called him Appleseed Man. The farmers and settlers welcomed him into their homes. They served him applesauce, fried apples, apple fritters, and apple dumplings. They showed him orchards of apple trees that had grown from the seeds he had given them.

Stop the next time you take a bite of a juicy apple. Think about the simple man who spent his lifetime sowing seeds across the country. A man who planted apple trees and understanding. You might even see the early morning smoke rising from his campfire. Bid him a good day if your paths happen to cross.

Name _____

Questions about
Johnny Appleseed

1. What work did Johnny Appleseed do?

_____

_____

2. Where was Johnny Appleseed's favorite place?

_____

_____

3. Johnny Appleseed didn't dig harbors like Paul Bunyan or ride twisters like Pecos Bill. What makes the story of his life a tall tale?

_____

_____

_____

4. What are some of the ways this tall tale suggested serving apples?

_____

_____

5. What's your favorite way to eat apples?

_____

_____

Name _____

Johnny Appleseed
Vocabulary

A. Write the number of each word on the line in front of its definition.

1. companion   _____ to scatter or plant

2. branched   _____ a friend

3. unconcerned   _____ an open area without trees

4. fritter   _____ a deep-dish fruit pie

5. sow   _____ a small fried cake containing sliced fruit

6. clearing   _____ to leave a main route and take a minor one

7. cobbler   _____ not worried

B. The tall tale says that Johnny Appleseed was an apple missionary. Look up the word **missionary**. Then tell how Johnny Appleseed could be considered a missionary.

_____

_____

_____

_____

_____

_____

_____

Name _____

Johnny Appleseed
Truth in a Tall Tale

Johnny Appleseed was born John Chapman. He was one of ten children. His father had a farm in Massachusetts. As a young man, Johnny moved to the Ohio River Valley. He began planting apple orchards in the wildernesses of Ohio, Indiana, and Illinois. In 1845, when John Chapman died, General Sam Houston recognized his work in a tribute before Congress.

The tale of Johnny Appleseed is based on historical facts about John Chapman.

List five things in the tale that could actually have happened.

_____

_____

_____

_____

_____

Write part of the tale that could <u>not</u> have actually happened.

_____

_____

_____

_____

Name _____

Johnny Appleseed
Reading Facts about Apples

Read the paragraph about apples and how they grow. Then mark the statements
true (T) or false (F).

Apple trees need fertile soil and lots of water to grow. The trees produce best when days are hot and nights are cool. During the growing season, buds form on the branches of an apple tree. These buds become blossoms and then apples. Today special apple trees in many orchards grow only about eight feet tall. They produce as many apples as their ancestors that grew about forty feet tall, but their apples are much easier to harvest.

_____ 1. Apple trees grow well in dry areas.

_____ 2. Apple trees produce well when days are hot and
nights are cool.

_____ 3. Each blossom on the tree can become an apple.

_____ 4. The smaller apple trees in today's orchards produce
fewer apples.

_____ 5. Apples from tall trees are harder to harvest than apples
from shorter trees.

_____ 6. Fertile soil is important to good apple production.

Annie Christmas—A Daring Rescue

Annie Christmas worked on the Mississippi River over a century ago. She spent her days on a keelboat carrying cotton, sugar, tobacco, lumber, and passengers up and down the river. This was unusual because for flatboats, a trip down the river was one-way. When the boat reached the mouth of the Mississippi, it was broken up and sold for lumber. Only Annie was strong enough to pole and haul her boat, *Big River's Daughter,* upriver against the current.

Now Annie was six feet eight inches tall. She weighed over 250 pounds. Her face was as black as the darkest, moonless night. Her eyes sparked with spirit. Annie respected the Mississippi, but she wasn't afraid of anything. It's said that she wore a necklace of freshwater pearls around her neck. She added one pearl every time she whipped a man in a fight. By the time she died, that necklace was over thirty feet long.

One time Annie decided to take the steamboat *Natchez Belle* down the river to New Orleans. She tied her keelboat to the stern of the paddlewheeler and strolled on board.

Soon after the steamboat began her trip, the weather turned. The skies filled with angry black clouds. The river became a wild beast. The captain of the *Natchez Belle* decided to use a new cutoff—a channel cut across a bend in the Mississippi—to return to New Orleans. Annie knew the big river. She knew that the cutoff was not fit for a steamboat like the *Belle.* She stormed to the pilothouse and yelled, "The cutoff is chock-full of snags and sandbars. Steer clear of that cutoff!"

Well, the captain was a stubborn man. He wasn't going to take the advice of any woman! He ordered Annie back to the deck and turned the *Belle* toward the cutoff. The passengers watched as the swirling, churning river boiled against the boat. The water was yellow with mud. Huge tree trunks floated by like soupbones in a stew. The driving wind and rain pounded down. Then, with a sickening thud, the steamboat ran aground on a sandbar. The wind and the river swallowed the cries of the frightened passengers. The steamboat reversed and pulled off the sandbar. It crashed into another sandbar just behind it. The ship shifted onto its side. The passengers clung to the rails above the raging yellow water.

Once again, Annie stomped off to the pilothouse. "Let me at that wheel. I'll take her back to the main channel. I know this here river!"

The captain drew his pistol and ordered her back to the deck. Annie glared at the captain and turned. The wind whipped wildly. Annie grabbed the rope that held her keelboat in tow. She pulled her boat closer and closer. The rain-soaked rope slipped between her hands, but she managed to pull it alongside.

"Come on board!" she bellowed to the passengers. "I'm steering back to the main channel. It's your only hope."

The passengers were afraid. The *Natchez Belle* shuddered and dipped farther to the side. The passengers scrambled onto the little flatboat. Annie cast off the towrope just as the steamboat's hull broke open.

Annie fought the current like a mother bear protecting her cubs. She clawed and snarled against the river. She poled the little keelboat back up the cutoff and turned into the main river channel. At that moment, the river calmed and welcomed her back. The passengers hugged Annie. They thanked her for saving their lives. Annie, a bit embarrassed by their gratitude, held the towrope between her teeth and jumped to the shore. "This boat's a-movin' too slow fer me!" she yelled. She tied the towrope around her waist and pulled. The boat flew along.

The passengers from the *Natchez Belle* reached New Orleans in record time, and the story of Annie's daring rescue became a legend up and down the big river.

Name _____

Questions about *Annie Christmas—* *A Daring Rescue*

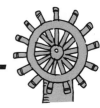

1. Why were Annie's keelboat trips up and down the Mississippi unusual?

_____

_____

2. What did Annie's pearls represent?

_____

_____

3. How did Annie react when the passengers thanked her after the rescue?

_____

_____

4. What was the name of Annie's keelboat?

_____

5. Does the keelboat's name reflect anything about Annie and her feelings about the Mississippi?

_____

_____

6. Why do you think Annie respected the river?

_____

_____

Name _____

Annie Christmas—A Daring Rescue
Analyzing Characters

List words that describe Annie.

_____

_____

_____

_____

Use your list to write a paragraph about Annie Christmas.

_____

_____

_____

_____

_____

List words that describe the captain of the *Natchez Belle.*

_____

_____

_____

_____

Use your list to write a sentence comparing the captain with Annie.

_____

_____

_____

_____

_____

Name _____

Annie Christmas—A Daring Rescue
Vocabulary

A. Write the number of each word on the line in front of its definition.

1. keelboat   _____ a line used in towing

2. steamboat   _____ a boat propelled by steam power

3. pole   _____ a long stick or staff

4. upriver   _____ toward the source of a river

5. downriver   _____ the deckhouse of a ship where navigating equipment is kept

6. longshoreman   _____ a shallow, covered riverboat that is poled or pulled

7. dock   _____ toward the mouth of a river

8. cutoff   _____ a worker who loads or unloads ships

9. channel   _____ a shortcut

10. sandbar   _____ a boat with a flat bottom for shallow waters

11. pilothouse   _____ a ridge of sand built up near the surface by water currents

12. towrope   _____ the deep part of a moving body of water where the main current flows

13. flatboat   _____ a place for loading and unloading ships

B. Choose three of the words above that are compound words. Then write what words were combined.

_____ = _____ + _____

_____ = _____ + _____

_____ = _____ + _____

Davy Crockett and Big Eater of the Forest

Sometimes Davy Crockett's bragging got him into trouble. Take the time he found himself in a thunderstorm in the middle of a forest with nothing but a stick. He had hiked ten miles. He was so hungry that he could have eaten any bear that wandered across his path. It was raining and the moon was hiding behind the clouds. Well, Davy began to search for something he could eat. He poked into a bush with his stick and pushed the branches aside. He saw two big yellow eyes staring at him. They were like a pair of burning coals ready to burst into flames.

Davy slapped his thigh in celebration. "Why, hello there. My name's Davy Crockett. I'm the biggest, strongest man this side of the Mississippi and I'm real hungry. I mean to eat you for my dinner!"

Thunder boomed as Davy spoke. A giant bolt of lightning lit the forest around him. Davy got a good look at his dinner. "Jumpin' Jezebel!"

Staring at Davy across the night was Big Eater of the Forest—the biggest panther ever seen in the frontier. The panther was just sittin' there. Spread around it like crumbs on a tablecloth were bones and skulls. Davy gulped. Before he could beg the varmint's pardon, the panther raised one paw. It swiped the air and the trees of the forest shook. The growl deep in its throat sounded like an approaching stampede.

"Hey, feller, I was just pokin' fun," Davy apologized and backed away slowly.

The panther shot white fire from his eyes and took a step toward Davy.

 Tall Tales • EMC 758

"Say there, feller, what say you and I...." But the panther just growled again and took one more step toward Davy. This time the growl echoed through the trees. Bears hibernating deep in their dens on the other side of the mountain woke up and sniffed the air.

"Well, now, I believe we could sing a duet," Davy teased. The panther roared again and the tops of the mountains shattered. Boulders rained down like a spring shower.

"Enough!" Davy shouted. "That's not a polite way of talkin'. I'm gonna get serious and you're gonna get some manners."

Davy crouched down. He began to grind his teeth. He growled his own growl. It was a growl so loud that it made the stars in the sky fall. The black night was awash with a storm of falling stars. Davy stepped toward the panther. They were both grinding and growling. They stared into each other's eyes. Then the two began wrestling for death or dinner.

The panther was about to crush Davy's head. Davy gave him a mighty blow under the chin. He grabbed the panther's tail and swung him 'round and 'round. He threw him to the ground and held him down with one foot. The panther yowled for mercy.

Davy took one step back. He pulled the panther up until he was staring into the once-burning eyes. "Okay, you yowler, you are a fine feller and a worthy foe. But the wild critters of the forest are not safe with you and your backwoods manners. Come home with me and I'll teach you a thing or two."

So Davy and Big Eater of the Forest became cozy companions. Davy taught the big black cat how to light the fire in the hearth with his burning eyes. The black cat plowed the fields with its mighty claws. The two of them spent their evenings growling duets into the still night air. If you're walking through the Tennessee woods late at night, you might hear them still.

Name _____

Questions about
Davy Crockett and Big Eater of the Forest

1. What is one thing that Davy Crockett did that got him into trouble? Use an example of this thing found in the story in your explanation.

_____

_____

_____

2. When did Davy get serious in his confrontation with the panther?

_____

_____

3. Was Davy surprised to see Big Eater of the Forest? How do you know?

_____

_____

4. If you had a cozy companion like Big Eater of the Forest, what would you teach it to do?

_____

_____

5. Exaggeration is an important part of tall tales. Give two examples of exaggeration that are found in this tale.

_____

_____

_____

Name _____

Davy Crockett and
Big Eater of the Forest
Vocabulary

Here is a list of verbs used in this tall tale. Write the number of each verb on the line in front of its meaning.

1. brag   _____ to break into small pieces

2. swipe   _____ to come toward

3. approach   _____ to bend low, ready to spring

4. grind   _____ to scuffle (fight)

5. hibernate   _____ to boast

6. shatter   _____ to strike out

7. crouch   _____ to spend the winter sleeping

8. wrestle   _____ to rub harshly

● ● ● Adding –ing ● ● ●

Add **-ing** to each of the verbs above. If the verb ends in a silent **e**, drop the **e** before adding **-ing**. If the verb is one syllable with a short vowel, double the final consonant before adding **-ing**.

_____   _____

_____   _____

_____   _____

_____   _____

                  Tall Tales • EMC 758

Name _____

Davy Crockett and
Big Eater of the Forest
Alliteration

Alliteration is the repetition of initial consonant sounds.

So Davy and Big Eater became **c**ozy **c**ompanions.

1. Writers use alliteration to emphasize a word, to name characters, and to add interest to their ideas. Write three examples of alliteration in this tall tale.

_____

_____

_____

2. Write an alliterative name for a wild critter that Davy might meet in his travels.

_____

● ● ● Tall Tale Speech ● ● ●

The dialect used in *Davy Crockett and Big Eater of the Forest* reflects the way that frontier woodsmen in Tennessee might have spoken when they told tales around the campfire. Often the final **g** in **-ing** words is dropped.

jumpin'   pokin'

Write a sentence in the tale's dialect using each verb below. Drop the final **g**.

1. walking _____

2. growling _____

3. wrestling _____

Name _____

Davy Crockett and Big Eater of the Forest
Similes

A. A **simile** makes a comparison by using the words **like** or **as**. Tell the two things being compared in each of the similes below.

1. They were like a pair of burning coals ready to burst into flames.

   _____   _____

2. Spread around it like crumbs on the tablecloth were bones and skulls.

   _____   _____

3. The growl deep in its throat sounded like an approaching stampede.

   _____   _____

4. Boulders rained down like a spring shower.

   _____   _____

B. Write similes of your own.

1. Compare Davy Crockett's strength with a modern machine.

   Davy Crockett was as strong as _____

   _____.

2. Compare the sound of Big Eater's growl with another scary sound.

   Big Eater's growl was like _____

   _____.

Old Pike and the Rattler

They say that long ago the prairie was covered with rattlesnakes. On a sunny day the snakes would come out to enjoy a sunbath. It looked like a giant serving of spaghetti on a flat plate. There were so many snakes that cowboys put their cattle on stilts to protect them from snakebites. But not all snakes were bad. The story of the prospector named Old Pike tells about one friendly rattler.

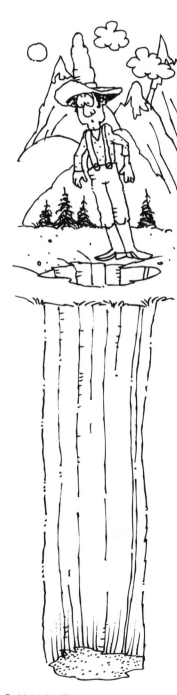

Old Pike was hired to inspect a deep mine shaft. Now he was as thin as a hollyhock stalk. The owner of the mine tied a rope to Pike's waist and lowered him down into the shaft. Pike was going down nicely when the rope snapped. Pike crashed to the bottom. The mine owner took one look down the shaft. He couldn't see anything. He yahooed three times. He couldn't hear anything. So he pulled up the broken rope and went home.

Pike had been knocked unconscious. When he came to at last, he looked up. He saw only a flicker of light from the opening far above him. There was no way for him to climb the steep walls. As Old Pike was considering what he could do, something fell from the top of the shaft. It bumped against the walls and landed at Old Pike's feet. Pike took a deep breath. It was a big rattlesnake—at least seven feet long. The fall had knocked it senseless.

Now Old Pike loved animals, even deadly rattlesnakes. He bent over and rubbed that scaly snake until it opened its eyes. As he rubbed the snake, he crooned soft, soothing sounds. He explained to the snake that he meant it no harm. Old Pike's gentle way charmed the snake. It coiled in his arms.

After a while the snake made up and down movements with its head. Old Pike guessed that the snake wanted to get out of the mine shaft. Now it was a long way to the top even for a strong, seven-foot-long rattlesnake. Old Pike bent low and gave the snake a giant boost. The snake sprung upward toward the rim of the shaft. The snake thrust its head out. Its fangs caught the wooden frame of the shaft. It hung for a moment and then hauled itself up and went wriggling out of sight.

Old Pike sat down. His new friend was gone. He was trapped at the bottom of the shaft. It was getting dark. The shadows were so thick that Old Pike pulled them around him like a blanket. He was hungry. He took out his knife and cut the heel off his boot. He chewed on the edge of the heel and pretended that it was a juicy piece of meat.

Then some pebbles fell on Pike's head. He looked up the shaft. A strong rope was coming down toward him. Old Pike thought the mine owner had come back for him. Then he looked again. The rope was the rattlesnake and a bunch of his friends. The rattlesnake had rounded up a rescue team. Old Pike grabbed the scaly rope and pulled himself out of the mine. When he got to the top he thanked his new friends.

Old Pike believed that rattlesnakes were man's best friends. You may not agree, but then have you ever been trapped at the bottom of a narrow mine shaft?

 Tall Tales • EMC 758

Name _____

Questions about
Old Pike and the Rattler

1. What was one of the dangers of the western frontier referred to in this tale?

   _____

2. What experience did Pike and the rattlesnake share?

   _____

3. List one event from the tale that supports each of these ideas.

   a. The way you feel may depend on the experiences you have had.

   _____

   _____

   b. Rattlesnakes aren't all bad.

   _____

   c. An animal can be more trustworthy than a human.

   _____

   _____

4. Explain how an experience you have had changed the way you think about something.

   _____

   _____

   _____

   _____

Name _____

Old Pike and the Rattler
Compound Words

A. Write the two words that were combined in each of these compound words from the story.

rattlesnake   _____   _____

snakebites   _____   _____

sunbath   _____   _____

cowboys   _____   _____

hollyhock   _____   _____

anything   _____   _____

B. Use the words above to complete these sentences.

1. _____ are responsible for their herds.

2. A _____ is a kind of flower.

3. The _____ is a reptile.

4. _____ can be deadly.

5. You can take a _____ without water.

Name _____

Old Pike and the Rattler
Vocabulary

Alliteration is the repeated use of an initial sound. Storytellers use alliteration to make their stories more interesting.

A. Underline the initial sound that is repeated in these sentences from *Old Pike and the Rattler*.

The rattlesnake had rounded up a rescue team.

He rubbed the snake and sang soft, soothing sounds.

B. Write several words that begin with the same sound as each word below.

mine	shaft	rope	boot
_____	_____	_____	_____
_____	_____	_____	_____
_____	_____	_____	_____
_____	_____	_____	_____

C. Choose one word. Using alliteration, write a sentence about that word.

_____

_____

_____

Name _____

Old Pike and the Rattler
Drawing What You Read

Draw a cartoon to illustrate each of these sentences.

On a sunny day the snakes would come out to enjoy a sunbath. It looked like a giant serving of spaghetti on a flat plate.

Old Pike grabbed the scaly rope and pulled himself out of the mine.

 Tall Tales • EMC 758

Mose, Volunteer Fireman

Mose was eight feet tall. He had hands as large as a first baseman's glove. His arms were so long that he could rub the back of his knees without bending over. When he laughed, tall buildings swayed as if in a storm. When he was angry, his shouting sounded like a trolley car rumbling over the rails. He wore a tall stovepipe hat over his flaming red hair.

One particular night while Mose was eating his dinner, the fire bell began to ring. Mose rushed to his station house. He pulled on his bright red shirt and his rainbow suspenders. He helped the other volunteer firemen move the fire machine to the doorway. The machine had no engine or horses to propel it. Mose and the other men grabbed the old pumper by two wooden bars. They pulled it through the streets to the fire.

The firemen ran down the narrow streets, lugging the heavy fire machine. Suddenly, in the street ahead, a horse-drawn trolley blocked their path. "Move out of the way! We're on our way to a fire!" Mose shouted.

"She won't budge!" the trolley driver yelled back. "She's stuck. One wheel is jammed between the tracks!"

"I'll take care of it!" Mose assured his men. He unhooked the horses from the trolley. He rolled up his sleeves and placed his huge hands under the car. Grunting and groaning, Mose lifted the trolley into the air. He carried it over his head like a waiter carries a tray in a fancy restaurant. The trolley passengers screamed. Mose staggered across the street. He slowly put the trolley back on its tracks. He wiped his hands and hurried back to his machine.

Once more the firemen raced through the streets toward the black clouds of smoke in the sky. When they arrived at the burning tenement, Mose hooked up the hose to the fire hydrant. His men began pumping the long handles on either side of the machine. The water began to shoot from the hose.

A woman ran up to Mose. "Help me! My baby's inside!" She pointed to a third-floor window. Mose grabbed a fire ladder. He balanced it on top of a barrel. He climbed toward the window. The ladder swayed to the left and to the right, but Mose kept on climbing. He hacked through the window with his ax and disappeared into the smoke and flames. Just then, the roof of the building collapsed.

"Mose will be trapped!" someone yelled.

Moments later Mose reappeared at the hacked-out window. He was covered with black soot. He started down the ladder, holding his stovepipe hat to his chest. Flames licked the ladder as he emerged from the smoke.

"He's alone!" cried the baby's mother. "Where is my baby?"

The ladder burst into flames and Mose jumped for the ground. The crowd rushed toward him. Mose pushed them back. He reached into his hat and pulled out a tiny crying infant. The baby's mother sobbed her thanks.

Mose doffed his hat and returned to his crew. "Just doing my duty, ma'am."

Mose Humphreys was a fearless fire fighter. He fought fires in a time when fire engines were only wagons with hoses. He and 4,000 other volunteer firemen pulled the wagons through the streets of New York. Mose became a folk hero during the mid-1800s when a play on Broadway, *A Glance at New York,* by B.A. Baker, featured him as its hero.

Tall Tales • EMC 758

Name _____

Questions about *Mose,* *Volunteer Fireman*

1. Some tall tales are told about characters that are based on real people. Who was Mose's character based on?

   _____

   _____

2. How was putting out fires different in 1850 from the way it is today?

   _____

   _____

   _____

3. What two accomplishments are described in this tale?

   _____

   _____

   _____

4. Would you like to work with someone like Mose? Tell why or why not.

   _____

   _____

   _____

   _____

   _____

Name _____

Mose, Volunteer Fireman
Vocabulary

Write the number of each word on the line in front of its definition.

1. suspenders   _____ to move

2. pumper   _____ straps used to keep pants up

3. trolley   _____ came out

4. staggered   _____ wept

5. tenement   _____ chopped

6. collapsed   _____ hurried

7. doffed   _____ came back

8. sobbed   _____ a machine used to force water through a hose

9. emerged   _____ fell down

10. reappeared   _____ took off (especially a hat)

11. hacked   _____ a crowded apartment building

12. raced   _____ moved forward unsteadily

13. blocked   _____ a wheeled vehicle

14. propel   _____ barred the way

                                       Tall Tales • EMC 758

Mose, Volunteer Fireman
Describing Words

A. Adjectives help the reader picture the characters and action in a story. Circle the adjectives in these phrases.

flaming red hair   tall stovepipe hat

tiny crying infant   horse-drawn trolley

B. Sometimes comparisons help readers picture what is happening. Tell what thing in the story is being described in each phrase.

1. as large as a first baseman's glove

_____

2. like a waiter carries a tray

_____

C. Use adjectives and comparisons to write your own descriptions.

1. a building that is on fire

_____

_____

2. a man who is strong

_____

_____

3. a mother who is frantic

_____

_____

Name _____

Mose, Volunteer Fireman
Using Quotation Marks

Quotation marks show the exact words of a speaker.

The trolley driver yelled, "She's stuck!"

Put the quotation marks in these sentences.

1. Move out of the way! We're on our way to a fire! Mose shouted.

2. I'll take care of it! Mose assured his men.

3. A woman ran up to Mose. Help me! My baby's inside! she screamed.

4. Mose doffed his hat and returned to his crew. Just doing my duty, ma'am.

5. Write a sentence using quotation marks to show what someone said.

_____

_____

_____

Jesse O

Jesse O grew up in Alabama, where his parents were sharecroppers. They planted and harvested crops on someone else's land for a share of the crop's profit. When he was a little boy, Jesse O was so sickly and thin that when he turned sideways he disappeared. Jesse ran through the fields and got thinner and thinner. Soon he was thinner than the tiny twigs on the willow tree that grew by the shack where he lived.

Jesse ran farther and farther each day. When he was nine, Jesse ran all the way to Ohio, pulling his family to a better life. It was there that he learned that "track" was more than stalking an animal.

Jesse was no longer a skinny kid who ran with the wind. He was like a powerful racing car. He ran so hard that the soles melted off his shoes. He jumped so high that the principal of his junior high school called him to get balls thrown onto the roof. Jesse ran and jumped himself into a legend.

You see, Jesse started running in track and field meets. He ran the 100-yard dash so quickly that the timers thought their watches were broken. Jesse piled up the victories. The pile of medals he won was so tall that even he couldn't jump over it. He broke so many records that the record keeper made a rubber stamp that said "Jesse O." That way, whenever Jesse set a new record, he could just stamp the name in the record book.

Jesse was so fast that his coaches had trouble locating him in the stadium. They finally put a spotter at each of his events. The spotter's job was to raise a banner when Jesse started competing. Sometimes Jesse finished one event and started another before the spotter at the first event could raise the banner!

Jesse O grew faster and stronger with every race he ran. Soon he was running 'round the world. He could finish a race in Berlin and make the start of the long jump in Chicago. As he ran, drops of sweat fell to the ground causing flash floods in Oklahoma. Sparks from his shoes started brush fires in Africa. TV weathermen gave Jesse O weather alerts so that those in his path could be prepared.

Jesse leaped across the Atlantic, and ocean liners were pulled into his wake. He broke every record there was to break. He ran every race there was to run. He even ran some races that weren't races yet.

Jesse O blazed a trail that runners today still follow. He ran so fast and so hard that he became a part of every track he ran on. If you are ever running and the wind is whistling by your ears, you may feel Jesse's hand in your own pulling you forward. His gentle voice may whisper words of encouragement. Jesse O ran his last race a long time ago. But he is still at every track. His skin is still as black as the cinders. His eyes are still as bright as the stars. His heart is still as big as the world he ran through many years ago.

     Tall Tales • EMC 758

Name _____

Questions about *Jesse O*

1. What does **track and field** mean as it is used in this tall tale?

_____

_____

2. How did the man in charge of records keep up with Jesse O?

_____

_____

3. How did Jesse's coaches find him in the stadium?

_____

_____

4. What potential dangers did Jesse pose for people in his path?

_____

_____

5. What were some of Jesse's accomplishments?

_____

_____

_____

6. Think of a nickname you might give Jesse O. Write it here.

_____

Name _____

Jesse O
Multiple-Meaning Words

Each of the words below has more than one correct meaning. Read the words and their meanings. Use these words to complete the sentences below. Then write the letter of the meaning you use on the line at the end of each sentence.

track

a. a prepared course for racing
b. an animal footprint

wake

a. a track left on the water by a ship
b. to cease sleeping

field

a. ground used for growing crops
b. an area for specific sports

stalk

a. to track
b. the stem of a plant

dash

a. a short, rapid run
b. a small amount

bank

a. a place to keep money
b. the edge of a river or stream

1. He stood on the _____ of the river while he fished. _____

2. The hunter will _____ the deer. _____

3. The farmer plowed the _____ before the rain. _____

4. Mom added a _____ of pepper to the soup. _____

5. Will he _____ when the alarm rings? _____

Name _____

Jesse O

Homonyms

Homonyms are words that sound the same but are spelled differently.

sole—soul   brake—break   raise—rays

Use the correct word in each sentence. Then illustrate the sentence with a cartoon drawing.

The _____ of his shoe had a hole in it.

The _____ of the sun melted the ice cream.

He will _____ the record for longest beard.

_____ the flag above your head.

Name _____

Jesse O

Writing Your Own Tall Tale

Many tall tales were inspired by real people. The tale of Jesse O is based on the life of Jesse Owens, a legend in American track and field. Here is a factual account of Jesse Owens' life.

> Jesse Owens was the son of Alabama sharecroppers. As a child he was skinny and often sick. When he was nine, his family moved to Ohio to find a better life. It was there, when he was in junior high school, Jesse met his mentor. Charles Riley was a gym teacher and coach of the track team. Coach Riley taught Jesse to run and jump. Jesse worked hard. He set his first track and field record in that same year. He ran the 100-yard dash in ten seconds flat. He went on to set many records in high school and college. At the 1936 Olympics in Berlin, Jesse won four gold medals as he set new world records in three events. One of the greatest track and field athletes of the United States, Jesse Owens began life as a poor, sickly boy and became a world hero.

1. List some of the things that happened in the tall tale about Jesse O that are based on actual events in Jesse Owens' life.

   _____   _____   _____

   _____   _____   _____

2. Name a famous sports figure.   _____

   List some of his or her accomplishments.

   _____   _____

   _____   _____

On another sheet of paper, write an original tall tale based on this sports figure.

Farmer Ted

Years ago, when a farmer was the power behind the plow, there was an ambitious farmer named Ted. Farmer Ted was not a big man in stature. He stood just as high as the garden gate. But Farmer Ted was a giant in determination, and he was determined to be a successful corn farmer.

Farmer Ted cleared a small plot of land between two winding creeks on the plains of Colorado. He carefully worked the ground until it was soft and ready for planting. Now since Ted was a careful farmer, you can be sure that he didn't just throw the corn seeds haphazardly into the field. No, he made small holes exactly one footstep apart and poked two seeds into each hole. Every day Farmer Ted checked his field. If the field was too dry, he carried water from the creeks and poured it onto the ground. If weeds were sprouting, he pulled the sprouts and gently patted the soil flat. If the field was too wet, he made little ditches between the rows to drain the extra water.

Before long, the corn sprouts poked their heads through the soil. They grew tall and strong. Farmer Ted continued his daily visits to the field. His vigilance and care paid off. The cornstalks grew taller and taller. Soon they were taller than the trees that grew along the creek bed. They were taller than the mountains that Farmer Ted could see against the horizon. Farmer Ted walked among the great stalks. He spent every day pulling sprouting weeds and carrying water from the creeks.

Now word spread across the plains about the diligent farmer and his amazing crop. People came from as far away as St. Louis to see the cornstalks that reached the sky. Farmer Ted felt like Jack with his giant beanstalk as he looked at his field.

The corn tasseled and giant ears nestled against the cornstalks. When the silk turned brown, Farmer Ted knew that it was time to harvest his crop. He climbed one stalk and sawed off an ear. The ear fell to the ground, shaking the leaves off the trees for miles around. Farmer Ted climbed back down and, with the help of several friends, husked the ear. The corn inside was as yellow as a dandelion. Each kernel was plump and begged to be eaten. Farmer Ted took one kernel and dropped it into a huge pot of boiling water. Within a few minutes the corn was ready. Farmer Ted sliced pieces off for everyone who lived nearby.

Farmer Ted's corn was delicious—the most delicious corn ever grown in Colorado. But there was one problem. Cutting off the single ear and cooking one kernel had taken Farmer Ted an entire day. How was he going to harvest his crop?

Farmer Ted sent out a call for help. Workers came from Wyoming and Utah and New Mexico. They drove across the mountains from Nevada and across the deserts from Arizona. They looked like tiny ants swarming over Farmer Ted's cornstalks. They harvested the corn. They piled the ears in huge yellow mountains. They felled the stalks and chopped them into silage. They hauled the corn to every farm and every granary in every state west of the Mississippi.

When there was just one stalk left in the field, Farmer Ted thanked the workers. He climbed the stalk for one last look at his cornfield. That was the last that anyone ever saw of Farmer Ted. Some people say that he simply climbed onto a sunbeam. He might have mistaken it for some of the sparkling silk from one of his giant corn ears. Others say that he had poured his whole heart into that corn crop. When the last stalk fell, there was simply nothing left of him. No one can say for sure, but his story lives on. Colorado corn farmers remember the little farmer with heart who grew corn that reached the sky.

131

Name _____

Questions about *Farmer Ted*

1. How was Farmer Ted's size different from his ambition?

_____

_____

2. What did Farmer Ted do to assure his crop's success?

_____

_____

_____

3. What makes this story a tall tale?

_____

_____

_____

4. What storybook character is compared to Farmer Ted? Explain what is alike about the two characters and what is different.

_____

_____

_____

_____

_____

Name _____

Farmer Ted
Corn Words

A. Label the picture to show that you understand what the words in the Word Box mean.

Word Box		
ear	stalk	silk
tassel	husk	kernel

B. Choose the synonyms for the underlined words in these sentences.

1. There was an <u>ambitious</u> farmer named Ted.

   ○ aspiring   ○ lazy   ○ wealthy

2. Farmer Ted was a giant in <u>determination</u>.

   ○ manners   ○ purpose   ○ intelligence

3. Word spread about the <u>diligent</u> farmer and his amazing crop.

   ○ poor   ○ wise   ○ hardworking

Name _____

Farmer Ted
Comparatives

When you add **-er** to an adjective you make a **comparative**. The new word compares two words.

A. Write the two things being compared in each of these sentences.

The corn was taller than the trees that grew along the creek bed.

_____   _____

The corn was taller than the mountains that Farmer Ted could see against the horizon.

_____   _____

B. Write sentences that compare the sizes of two things. Use these comparatives.

shorter _____

_____

wider _____

_____

faster _____

_____

cleaner _____

_____

Name _____

Farmer Ted
Creative Writing

Ted is really a Colorado corn farmer. He is short and he is hardworking. *Farmer Ted* is based on a few things that are true. Then part of the truth is exaggerated and the story becomes a tall tale.

Choose someone you know to write a story about. Write down a few characteristics that will remain the same in the story. Write down some characteristics or events that you will exaggerate. Give the character a name.

The character's name: _____

Characteristics that will remain the same

_____

_____

_____

_____

Characteristics that will be exaggerated

_____

_____

_____

_____

What events will be included in the story?

_____

_____

_____

_____

_____

_____

On another sheet of paper, write a tall tale about your character.

   Tall Tales • EMC 758

Answer Key

Page 6
1. Sooner Hound liked to run. He ran very fast and never got tired.
2. Sooner Hound had long thin legs, bright red spots, and his long tail had a curl in the middle.
3. Sooner Hound raced the train and won.
4. Explanations will vary. Students' answers should include the idea that "inseparable pair" means that they were always together. The tale says that wherever Red's engine went, Sooner Hound ran alongside.

Page 7
A. 1. grand father   4. station master
   2. along side   5. rail road
   3. some times
B. 1. Sometimes, stationmaster
   2. railroad
   3. grandfather, alongside
C. Sentences will vary.

Page 8
A. Sooner Hound's ears, pendulum of a clock
B. Exact wording of the sentences will vary.
   1. Sooner Hound had so many spots he looked like he had the measles.
   2. Sooner Hound's tail looked like an *e* scribbled on the chalkboard.
   3. Sooner Hound's legs were so long it looked like he was standing on stilts.
   4. Sooner Hound ran as fast as a space shuttle bursting through the atmosphere.

Page 9
A. 1. "Shucks!" Red replied. "Sooner doesn't ride. He just runs along beside the train!"
   2. "Oh, no!" Red answered. "Most of the time he runs up ahead of it."
   3. "Suits me," said Red. "But I have to warn you, Sooner is the fastest thing on four legs."
   4. The new stationmaster said, "Hey there, Red. It's against the rules for a dog to ride on the train."
B. Sentences will vary.
   Mom said, "Don't forget to lock the door when you go out."
C. stationmaster
   Red
   stationmaster
   Red

Page 12
1. Joe and Bess were brother and sister and they were both very strong.
2. The Englishman wanted to wrestle with Joe.
3. The Englishman was persistent. He didn't give up when he found out how strong Joe was. He trained harder and returned to wrestle Joe.
4. Students' opinions will vary. A sample answer might be: I don't think Bess was calm. The Englishman chuckled and she got so mad that she threw him and his horse over the fence.
5. Bess lifted the plow to check the blade, and she threw the Englishman and his horse over a fence.

Page 13
A. 3
   5
   4
   1
   2
B. Students' definitions will vary.
   1. turned around
   2. a little sick
   3. was shocked or surprised

Page 14
A. 1. synonyms from the tale— whispered, agreed, announced, murmured, shouted, confided
   2. Students should list four additional synonyms.
B. Students' word choices for completing the sentence will vary.
C. Students' responses will vary, but should indicate that the meaning can change. Example: Yes, the meaning changes. For example, there is a big difference between whispering something and shouting something.

Page 15
1. making a decision, a wrestling match
2. Students' responses may vary. Examples:
   Similarities—wrestling and deciding something can both be hard work. There are two participants in a wrestling match; there are usually two choices involved in making a decision. Sometimes you are prepared and sometimes you are not. In wrestling the competitors struggle back and

forth with one having the advantage and then the other; in deciding something, sometimes one idea seems better and then the other idea seems better.

   Differences—Wrestling is physical work; deciding is mental work. You wrestle on a mat; you decide something anywhere. There's a referee in a wrestling match; you usually decide something by yourself. Wrestling is usually a male event; decision making is done by everyone.
3. Students' original examples will vary.

Page 18
1. Pecos Bill was raised by a coyote.
2. Bill bounced out of his parent's wagon just before it crossed the Pecos River and was lost. Whenever his parents thought of him they thought of the river too, so they called him Pecos Bill.
3. The coyote taught Pecos Bill all the ways of the wilderness—the secrets of hunting, how to leap long distances and run without getting tired, and how to talk to other animals.
4. When Pecos Bill drank from a stream after he had met a man, he saw his reflection and realized that he was a man too.
5. The cowboy who discovered Bill was one of Bill's brothers. They met by the edge of the Pecos River, the same river where Bill had been lost many years before.

Page 19
A. 4
   1
   5
   3
   7
   6
   2
B. 1. loaded
   2. long
   3. uncombed
   4. lost

Page 20
Students' responses will vary.

Page 21

5
6
1
4
2
7
3
8

Page 24

1. a tornado
2. The tall tale compares a bucking bronco to the tornado. It says that the twister cakewalked and bucked and turned. Those are all terms used to describe horses.
3. the Grand Canyon and Death Valley
4. Students' responses may vary, but should include riding and roping.
5. Widow Maker—The horse was probably named Widow Maker because it was so dangerous that it "made widows" when it bucked off and killed the men who tried to ride it.
6. Students' answers will vary. For example—I think that Pecos Bill would have to have been an amazing cowboy. Can you imagine being able to lasso a river and tip it to pour the water out? Riding the tornado would be an incredible experience. I don't believe that Pecos Bill could have been real, but he certainly was the *gall-darndest*!

Page 25

A. 3
6
2
5
1
4

B. Students' responses will vary. For example:
1. I can put my work away quick as a wink.
2. I would leap headlong into the new play.
3. I would shy away from a lizard on the sidewalk.

Page 26

1. bucked and spun around—bucking bronco
2. got onto—horse
3. went over the edge—water
4. rose up—horse

Page 27

Page 30

1. Sue wanted a brand-new, store-bought wedding dress with a bustle, and she wanted to ride Bill's horse to the wedding.
2. A widow is a woman whose husband is dead. Bill's horse must have killed a cowboy and earned the name Widow Maker.
3. Sue was bucked off and blasted into space. Then her bustle made her bounce many times.
4. Texas was in the middle of a drought. It was so dry that children didn't know what rain was. It was so dry that spit disappeared before it ever hit the ground. It was so dry that cattle walked around with their tongues hanging out.
5. Sue's Plan:
   • Bill would lasso the Little Dipper.
   • Sue and Bill would pull on the rope and tip the dipper.
   • The water from the dipper would fall on Texas.

Page 31

A. 9
1
5
2
7
6
4
8
3

B. 1. proposed
2. bustle
3. solution, drought
4. lasso, constellation

Page 32

A. Pecos Bill—3, 7
Slue-Foot Sue—1, 4, 5, 8
Widow Maker—2, 6

B. Students' sentences will vary.

Page 33

A. 1. The size of the catfish would have to be exaggerated if a person were going to ride it.
2. Sue's fall off the horse was exaggerated. A horse, even Widow Maker, could not buck you into space.
3. The length of the drought was exaggerated. It would be very unusual to not have any rain for several years.
4. Bill's skill with the lasso and the length of his rope were exaggerated. It would be impossible to lasso something so far away.

B. Students' responses will vary.

Page 36

1. The tale takes place on a small farm on the coast of California. Although the teller doesn't give an exact time, the events seem to be contemporary.
2. The problem is that Little Sir crows too loudly.
3. Students should list three of the following:
   • Little Sir's crow was so loud that Farmer Dave had to sleep in a soundproof room.
   • It was so loud that librarians complained about the noise.
   • A morning noise alert was issued for the California Coast.
   • People in Wyoming woke up to Little Sir's crow.
   • Farmer Dave's neighbors wanted to sell their farms.
4. Farmer Dave talked with Little Sir and found out that he didn't like being called "little." He began to call him "Big Sir."
5. They both lived happily on the farm. Big Sir got the respect that he wanted, and Dave had the complete farm he wanted.

Page 37

A. 6
5
1
7
8
3
2
4

B. 1. protect or preen
2. strut
3. count on
4. complain

Page 38

Students' responses will vary.

Things that probably wouldn't happen because of a rooster's crow:
a farmer's hearing being damaged
television crews visiting a farm
librarians complaining
a noise alert being issued
people in Wyoming waking up to the crow
ships being saved

Things that might actually happen:
a farmer might buy a rooster
a rooster would strut, preen, and crow
a rooster would scratch at the gravel and sit on a perch
neighbors might be annoyed with early morning crowing
the farmer would care for the rooster
the farmer could name the rooster Little Sir
someone might take offense at being called "little"

Page 39

Students' sequels will vary.

Page 42

1. Stormalong loved the ocean. He lived beside it, watched it continually, and as a baby learned skills a sailor would use like tying knots. The tale says that Stormalong breathed in so much ocean spray that he had ocean water in his veins. He watched the waves so long that his brown eyes turned to the sea's blue-gray.
2. 12 feet tall
3. He couldn't stand too close to the ship's rail or the ship would list. He had to sleep in an extra-large lifeboat because a sailor's hammock wasn't long enough. He had to watch his appetite.
4. Stormalong tied the kracken's arms into knots.

5. Students' responses will vary. One example might be: Stormalong was a good problem-solver. When one solution didn't seem to be working, he thought of another and tried it. His wrestling match with the kracken is a good example of that problem-solving. When whacking off the kracken's arms with the cleaver didn't work, he decided to tie the arms into knots.
6. A.B., are Alfred Bulltop Stormalong's first two initials, so when Stormalong signed his name on the ship's register "Stormalong, A.B.," he was simply signing his name. The tag line says that Stormalong was an Able-Bodied Seaman. When sailors today sign their names followed by A.B., it must stand for "able-bodied."

Page 43

b
l
g
j
a
e
n
h
c
m
i
d
f
k

Page 44

Students' definitions will vary.
"Signed on board" means agreed to work as a part of the ship's crew.
"Happier than a sheephead in a school of sardines" means very happy.
"Stopped rock-still" means motionless like a rock.
To bite something "clean through" is to sever it completely.
"Then and there" means at that time and place.

Page 45

1. The ship would tip to the side where he was standing.
2. Stormalong had ocean water in his veins.
3. Stormalong's eyes turned from brown to blue-gray.
4. The wrestling match caused towering waves.
5. The monster rolled away.

Page 48

1. Paul was born on the Fourth of July.
2. Paul pulled up the neighbor's trees and put them in his father's lumber wagon when he imitated his father's work.
3. Paul's parents anchored his cradle in the harbor. Paul got tired of watching the gulls and rocked the cradle back and forth so hard that the town flooded.
4. Paul raced with the deer, wrestled with the grizzlies, and grew.
5. Paul lifted Babe each morning when he hugged the ox. Lifting the growing ox was like weight lifting and helped Paul get stronger.
6. Paul wanted to make a life of his own. He left home to clear forests and make way for settlers moving west.

Page 49

1. a. yes
   b. Sentences will vary. One example: When my little brother was a toddler, he fell down all the time.
2. a. yes
   b. Sentences will vary. One example: The boy's report card was distressing to his mother.
3. a. no
   b. Sentences will vary. One example: The fisherman anchored his boat before he cast out his line.
4. a. no
   b. Sentences will vary. One example: The puppies wrestled in the dry leaves.

Page 50

	Paul Bunyan	(student info)
Birthday	July 4th	(student info)
Birth Weight	156 pounds	(student info)
Father's Occupation	logger	(student info)
Favorite Things to Do	race deer, wrestle grizzlies	(student info)
Pets	Babe, the Blue Ox	(student info)

Page 51

Events that students include on the time line may vary, but should include the following:

Paul's birthday on July 4 (on the bottom)

Paul pulling up neighbors' trees

Paul rocking the cradle in the harbor

Paul living in the wilderness

Paul finding a blue ox in the snow

Paul taking the ox home and naming it Babe

Paul and Babe leave home (on top)

Page 54

1. Babe was blue. Babe was big.
2. Babe couldn't find enough to eat or drink.
3. Paul and Babe traveled to eastern Washington to find water. Babe found a mighty river and drank it dry.
4. a. false—Students' justifications will vary. An ox cannot be 162 feet wide between the eyes. A big ox might measure 1 foot.
   b. true—Students' justifications will vary. Powerful rivers do rush over waterfalls. Niagara Falls is a good example.
   c. false—Students' justifications will vary. A single ox would not be able to drink enough water to diminish a raging river.
   d. false—Students' justifications will vary. Eastern Washington is across the United States from New York City. Babe's bellow could not be heard that far away.

Page 55

A. 1. down/stream
   2. sand/bar
   3. sage/brush
   4. hind/quarters
   5. sun/light
   6. knee/deep
   7. shore/line

   2
   7
   5
   3
   4
   6
   1

B. 1. downstream
   2. sandbar
   3. shoreline
   4. knee-deep
   5. sagebrush

Page 56

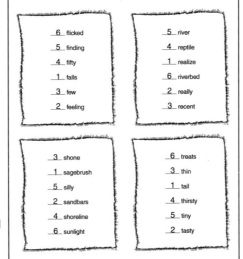

6 flicked	5 river
5 finding	4 reptile
4 fifty	1 realize
1 falls	6 riverbed
3 few	2 really
2 feeling	3 recent

3 shone	6 treats
1 sagebrush	3 thin
5 silly	1 tail
2 sandbars	4 thirsty
4 shoreline	5 tiny
6 sunlight	2 tasty

Page 57

Students' responses will vary.

Page 60

1. Babe was sick and Paul thought that Pacific whales' milk might help save Babe.
2. Paul was digging a grave for Babe. When Babe recovered, Paul finished the hole to make a new harbor for Seattle.
3. Mt. Rainier and Mt. Baker are the piles of dirt and rocks that Paul dug out of the sound.
4. The people of Whidbey were self-centered. They wanted to have the sound named after them.
5. Paul wanted to please all of the people.

Page 61

A. sound—5, 8
   canal—1, 4
   harbor—2, 9
   peninsula—7
   mainland—6
   passage—3
B. 1. Sound
   2. harbor
   3. mainland

Page 62

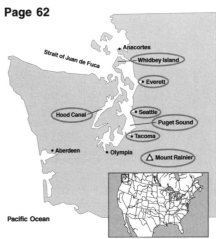

Page 63

1. Paul started digging Puget Sound as a grave for Babe the Blue Ox and completed it when Peter Puget suggested making a harbor for Seattle.
2. Mount Rainier is the pile of sediment and soil that Paul dug up as he created the sound.
3. Hood Canal was Paul's answer to some folks who wanted a harbor.
4. Paul threw shovel after shovel of dirt back into the channel when he became angry with the people of Whidbey Peninsula. This dirt became the islands.
5. Paul used his pickax to separate Whidbey Peninsula from the mainland, creating an island.

Page 66

1. Paul Bunyan's cook probably got his name because he loved to make pea soup.
2. He used up all the peas in his part of the country.
3. Shorty tried using BB shot painted green instead of peas, but it didn't work. When the men ate the soup, the BBs made them so heavy they couldn't do their work.
4. Shorty got peas from a farmer on the other side of the country. The wagon carrying the peas got stuck and the peas rolled into a lake. Even though this solution seemed to be a failure, it wasn't. The lake turned out to be a hot springs and cooked the peas, making a lake full of soup.
5. Babe knew that making soup in the lake had happened by accident.

Tall Tales • EMC 758

Page 67

A. 2
4
1
6
3
5

B. Students' explanations will vary.
1. very sad
2. bountiful or very successful crop
3. enough to serve everyone

Page 68

7
4
2
1
3
5
6

Students' drawings will vary.

Page 69

1. Paul had to feed a lot of hungry lumberjacks.
2. The men liked Shorty's soup and he always had a pot ready to serve.
3. Shorty tried to substitute BBs for peas.
4. The peas rolled out of the wagon and into the lake. They cooked in the hot water.
5. He had a never-ending supply of delicious pea soup.

Page 72

1. John liked to do work with a hammer.
2. He tried plowing fields, picking cotton, and poling barges.
3. John was upset when the man running the drill bragged that it could outwork seven men.
4. Many people were moving westward to start new lives.
5. John Henry won the contest because the drill broke down.
6. The storyteller wants to emphasize that John Henry's life and death were about hammering. The hammer was a part of John Henry like an arm or a foot.

Page 73

A.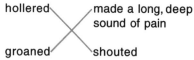
exclaimed — cried out with surprise
bragged — boasted
hollered — shouted
groaned — made a long, deep sound of pain

B. bragged
exclaimed
hollered
groaned

C. got his dander up — made him angry
plumb worn out — exhausted
'tweren't — it wasn't
set out — made a start

Page 74

1. noun, soil or earth
2. verb, crushed
3. verb, make a hole
4. noun, a pointed tool used for boring holes
5. noun, a tool with a heavy metal head
6. verb, strike loudly

Page 75

Students' phrases will vary. Examples of adjectives follow:
heavy, hard hammer
dangerous, digging drill
transcontinental train track
mighty, monstrous mountain
stark, still statue

Page 78

1. They remember Joe Magarac as the greatest steelworker that ever lived. He worked night and day.
2. "Magarac" means jackass. A jackass is a male donkey. Donkeys were used for work because they were strong, steady workers. Joe Magarac said that he was like a jackass because all he did was eat and work. He was certainly strong.
3. The tale says that he was her favorite and that everyone knew she hoped he would be declared the winner. She gave him a geranium. When Pete was beaten by Joe, she looked back longingly at Pete.
4. While Joe won the contest, he turned down the prize. He chose to work and eat.
5. Students' answers will vary. An example might be, Joe was like a machine because he only stopped for fuel (food).

Page 79

6
2
1
3
4
8
7
5
9
10

Page 80

A. 1. sky, fire—metaphor
2. Pete's face, red silk dress—simile
3. Joe's back, ore car—simile
4. Joe's wrists, steel drums—simile
5. Joe's chest, polished steel—simile

B. Students' responses will vary.

Page 81

①, 8
2, ⑪
10, ⑫
3, ⑨
5, ⑥
④, 7

Page 84

1. Examples will vary.
a good shot—yes—He won the shooting contest as a boy.
soft-spoken and humble—no—Mike bellowed, "I can out-run, out-shoot, out-fight, and out-brag anyone on this here river!"
strong and determined—yes—Mike had a cap full of red feathers indicating that he was strong and tough. He didn't let the older men in the shooting contest scare him.
2. Mike shot off the mosquito's stinger.
3. He decided that he wanted to learn a trade.
4. Mighty Marksman

Page 85

A. braggin' — jumpin'
leapin' — boastin'
whoopin' — hollerin'

B. riverboat words
keelboat
poling it up and down
captain
docks

shooting words
bull's-eye
target
marksman
aim

Page 86
1. stopped
2. doubted Mike could win the contest
3. wouldn't annoy me
4. boasted about their strength
5. bragging
6. Sentences will vary.

Page 87
Students' responses will vary. Some possible responses are:
Similarities—both were good marksmen, won shooting contests as young men, five shots in the contest, became captains of keelboats

Differences—real Mike didn't shoot stinger off a mosquito, Mike in the tale did a lot more whoopin' and braggin'

Page 90
1. The story is set at the time when there were trappers and traders and when men and women were traveling west to seek their fortunes. Sal Fink lived in a cabin in Kentucky.
2. She was in the forest hunting wildcats.
3. attacked
4. There were too many men for her to get away.
5. a fearless frontierswoman
6. Sal Fink could yell in Minneapolis and the people in New Orleans could hear her. It is because of her loud whoops that she became known as "The Screamer."

Page 91
Students' definitions and sentences may vary. Some possible responses follow:
1. wanted to—Sal let out a whoop whenever she wanted to.
2. spirit, determination—She had spirit as well as looks.
3. tied up tight—The pirates tied Sal up tight.

4. waited patiently—Sal waited patiently while the pirates argued.
5. the right amount of sleep—A lady has to have the right amount of sleep.

Page 92
8
4
6
1
3
7
5
2

Page 93
Sal—mother bear
pirates tied up—bunch of bananas
Students' illustrations will vary.

Page 96
1. The story says that he was an apple missionary. He was a teacher. He taught settlers how to plant seeds. He was a naturalist. He lived among the animals and studied them.
2. Johnny Appleseed loved apple orchards and the wilderness. He spent lots of time in the forest with the animals.
3. Students' responses will vary. One response might be:
Imagine a man who talked with the animals, walked barefoot through the wilderness, never killed a living thing, and single-handedly planted apple orchards across the United States. That man became a folk hero. As his story was told over and over, it became more exaggerated and soon *Johnny Appleseed* became a tall tale.
4. pies, jams, cobblers, salads, applesauce, fried apples, apple fritters, and apple dumplings
5. Students' responses will vary.

Page 97
A. 5
1
6
7
4
2
3

B. Students' responses will vary. One possible response follows:
A missionary is a person who spreads the gospel of a religion to the people. Johnny Appleseed didn't spread the gospel of any official religion, but he did spread his peaceful ways, the idea of tolerance, his appreciation of nature, and his apple seeds to all the people of the frontier.

Page 98
Students' responses will vary. Some possible responses include:
Could actually happen—collect and plant apple seeds, travel in a canoe, camp in the wilderness, wear clothes made from a flour sack, read the Bible to animals, and watch the country grow

Could not happen—wrestle with a bear cub while the mother watched

Page 99
1. F
2. T
3. T
4. F
5. T
6. T

Page 103
1. Usually keelboats went only downriver and were sold at the mouth of the Mississippi. Annie was so strong that she poled her keelboat upriver, as well as downriver.
2. Annie added a pearl to her necklace each time she whipped a man in a fight.
3. Annie was embarrassed. She jumped off the boat and pulled it along with a towrope.
4. *Big River's Daughter*
5. Students' responses will vary. One possible response might be: Yes, I think Annie named her keelboat *Big River's Daughter* because she saw herself as a daughter of the river.
6. Students' responses will vary. One possible response might be: Annie respected the river because she understood its power.

Page 104

Students' responses will vary.
Annie—strong, spirited, industrious, brave, determined, humble
Annie Christmas was a strong, determined keelboat captain. She was as spirited as the Mississippi River where she spent her days. In a time when only men were keelboat captains, she became a legend.

Captain of the *Natchez Belle*—stubborn, prejudiced, would rather be dead than wrong
Both Annie and the captain of the *Natchez Belle* piloted their boats down the Mississippi, but Annie knew the river and better understood its dangers.

Page 105
A. 12
2
3
4
11
1
5
6
8
13
10
9
7
B. Students may choose keelboat, steamboat, upriver, downriver, longshoreman, cutoff, sandbar, pilothouse, towrope, or flatboat.

Page 108
1. Students' responses may vary. One possible response is: Davy poked in the bush looking for something to eat. He disturbed the panther and then had to figure out a way to save himself.
2. As Davy tried to back away from the panther, the panther continued to roar. When boulders rained down on his head after one of the panther's giant roars, Davy told the panther that he was going to get serious and teach the big cat some manners.
3. Davy was surprised. When he got a good look at the panther, he exclaimed, "Jumpin' Jezebel!"
4. Students' responses will vary.

5. Students' responses will vary. Two possible responses might be: The panther's growl is exaggerated. The storyteller says that bears hibernating deep in their dens on the other side of the mountain woke up and sniffed the air when they heard the growl. Davy's growl is exaggerated too. The storyteller says that Davy's growl made the stars in the sky fall.

Page 109
6
3
7
8
1
2
5
4

bragging
swiping
approaching
grinding
hibernating
shattering
crouching
wrestling

Page 110
1. Students' responses may vary. Three possible responses are: Jumpin' Jezebel
grinding and growling
fine feller, foe
2. Alliterative names will vary.

Students' sentences will vary.
Examples:
1. I was walkin' down the road when I saw the car.
2. The dog was growlin' at the moon.
3. My brother is always wrestlin'.

Page 111
A. 1. panther's eyes, burning coals
2. bones and skulls, crumbs on a tablecloth
3. panther's growl, an approaching stampede
4. rockslide, spring shower
B. Students' responses will vary.
1. Davy Crockett was as strong as a powerful land mover rumbling forward with its load.
2. Big Eater's growl was like a hurricane slashing rain and wind.

Page 114
1. rattlesnakes
2. They had both fallen down the mine shaft.
3. Students' responses may vary. Possible responses might be:
a. Pike believed that rattlesnakes were man's best friends as a result of his experiences with the snake in the mine shaft.
b. The rattlesnake rescue team helped save Pike.
c. The mine owner left Pike for dead, but the rattlesnake enlisted the help of its friends to save Pike.
4. Students' responses will vary.

Page 115
A. rattle snake
snake bites
sun bath
cow boys
holly hock
any thing
B. 1. Cowboys
2. hollyhock
3. rattlesnake
4. Snakebites
5. sunbath

Page 116
A. The <u>r</u>attlesnake had <u>r</u>ounded up a <u>r</u>escue team.
He rubbed the <u>s</u>nake and <u>s</u>ang <u>s</u>oft, <u>s</u>oothing <u>s</u>ounds.
B. Students' responses will vary.
C. Students' responses will vary. For example: Many mines seem mysterious.

Page 117
Students' cartoons will vary.

Page 120
1. The character is based on Mose Humphreys, a volunteer fireman in New York City in the mid-1800s.
2. In the 1800s the firemen were volunteers. They pulled their pumpers through the streets.
3. The tale describes how Mose moved a trolley stuck in its tracks and rescued a baby on the third floor of a burning building.
4. Students' responses will vary. They may reference the fact that Mose was fearless, powerful, a good problem solver, and humble.

Page 121
14
1
9
8
11
12
10
2
6
7
5
4
3
13

Page 122
A. (flaming) (red) hair
(tiny) (crying) infant
(tall) (stovepipe) hat
(horse-drawn) trolley
B. 1. Mose's hands
2. the way that Mose lifted and carried the trolley
C. Students' responses will vary.

Page 123
1. "Move out of the way! We're on our way to a fire!" Mose shouted.
2. "I'll take care of it!" Mose assured his men.
3. A woman ran up to Mose. "Help me! My baby's inside!" she screamed.
4. Mose doffed his hat and returned to his crew. "Just doing my duty, ma'am."
5. Students' responses will vary.

Page 126
1. Track and field is a group of running and throwing events usually held at a track meet. The events might include pole vaulting, broad jumping, dashes, and relays.
2. The tale says that he had a rubber stamp with Jesse's name on it so he could just stamp the name instead of writing it.
3. They put spotters at different events. Whenever Jesse was competing, the spotter at that event would raise a banner.
4. Drops of sweat caused flash floods in Oklahoma, sparks from his shoes started brush fires in Africa, and ocean liners were pulled into his wake.

5. Students' responses may vary. Jesse set many world records. He proved that a sickly boy from a poor family could become a champion.
6. Students' nicknames will vary. One example might be The Streak.

Page 127
1. bank, b
2. stalk, a
3. field, a
4. dash, b
5. wake, b

Page 128
sole, rays
break, Raise
Students' drawings will vary.

Page 129
1. Students' responses will vary. They might include:
Jesse Owens was skinny and sick and came from a poor family.
Jesse Owens moved to Ohio as a young boy.
Jesse Owens learned to run in junior high school and started breaking records.
Jesse Owens became a track and field hero.
2. Students will choose different sports figures to analyze and write about.

Page 132
1. Farmer Ted was a short man, but he had tall ambitions.
2. Farmer Ted worked hard. He prepared the ground carefully, measured the distance between the seeds he planted, and checked his field every day. He watered and weeded and drained his field when necessary.
3. Students' opinions may vary, but should reflect the use of exaggeration.
4. Students' responses may vary. They might include some of the following information:
Farmer Ted is compared to Jack in the tale *Jack and the Beanstalk.* Both characters planted seeds that grew into towering plants. Both climbed their plants and benefited from their crops.

Farmer Ted grew corn and was a careful, diligent farmer. Jack grew magic beans and simply tossed the seeds out of the window. In the end Farmer Ted climbed up the cornstalk and disappeared, while Jack climbed down his beanstalk and lived happily ever after.

Page 133
A.

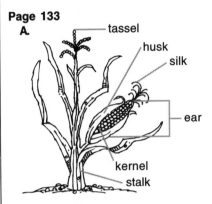

tassel
husk
silk
ear
kernel
stalk

B. 1. aspiring
2. purpose
3. hardworking

Page 134
A. corn—trees
corn—mountains
B. Students' comparisons will vary.

Page 135
Students' creative writing will vary.